I0711166

AMERICAN VIRTUE

CAPITALISM
and
SOCIAL PROGRAMS

VS

CORPORATISM
and
SOCIALISM

D.W. Cox

RoseDog Books
PITTSBURGH, PENNSYLVANIA 15238

The contents of this work including, but not limited to, the accuracy of events, people, and places depicted; opinions expressed; permission to use previously published materials included; and any advice given or actions advocated are solely the responsibility of the author, who assumes all liability for said work and indemnifies the publisher against any claims stemming from publication of the work.

All Rights Reserved
Copyright © 2020 by D.W. Cox

No part of this book may be reproduced or transmitted, downloaded, distributed, reverse engineered, or stored in or introduced into any information storage and retrieval system, in any form or by any means, including photocopying and recording, whether electronic or mechanical, now known or hereinafter invented without permission in writing from the publisher.

RoseDog Books
585 Alpha Drive, Suite 103
Pittsburgh, PA 15238
Visit our website at www.rosedogbookstore.com

ISBN: 978-1-6461-0352-2
eISBN: 978-1-6461-0398-0

Contents

Preface vii

Introduction xi

Chp. 1 American Governance 1

Psychology and Government 1

Documents of our Virtue 3

Freedom Leads to Wealth 4

Economic Policy and Criminality .6

Consumers vs. State 8

Decentralization vs. Centralization 10

A Guarantee of Opportunity...Not Success 11

Collectivism...It Doesn't Work 12

Chp. 2 The U.S. Constitution: A Standard for the World 15

Church and State 15

UN Law vs. the U.S. Constitution 16

U.S. Constitution vs. Sharia 17

A Flawed World Agenda 19

Capitalism vs. Corporatism 20

A Modern Pathological Work Culture 22

Chp. 3 Globalism's Ultimate Failure **25**
Economic Philosophy 101 25
Marxism 26
U.S. Constitution under Attack 29
Socialism and Centralization 31
Socialism, Faith, and Merit 33
Socialism and Education 36

Chp. 4 The Danger of Modern Liberalism **39**
Take Care of Us 39
Intellectualism 42
Alinsky and Community Organizing 44
ANTIFA, Nazism, and Socialism 47

Chp. 5 Communications Breakdown **51**
A Global Shockwave 51
Propaganda vs. Journalism 52
Ethics, Media and Youth 53
The Entertainment Industry 54
Free Will and Choice 55

Chp. 6 Academics in Regression **57**
Secular Teaching 57
Attitude and Social Extremes 58
Curricular Integrity and Extremism 60
Learning 61
Competence in Perspective 62

Chp. 7 History: A Broken Time Capsule **65**
History and Interpretation 65
History and Academia 66
Limits of Ancient Records Acquisition 67

Addressing Historical Revisionism 68

Chp. 8 Law and Disorder **73**
The Great Charter of the Liberties 73
What is Law? 73
Questionable Legal Practices 74
The Science of Logic 75
Anarchy and Lawlessness 76

Chp. 9 Politics of Faith and Fear **79**
The Eternal Sea 79
Politics Defined 80
Organizations are Inevitable 80
Extreme Organizations 81

Chp. 10 Free Will and Extremism **83**
Choice and the Origins of Extremism 83
Extremes in Science 84
Extremes in Religion 86
Fundamentalism is Not Spirituality .87
The Roots of Terrorism 88
Freedom and Free Will 89
Nature, Nurture and Free Will 89

Epilogue **93**

Appendix **97**

Bibliography **111**

Preface

The fundamentals of America's political-economic system and its success is contingent on the virtue of the people. We are now at crossroads with choosing the path of virtue or vice. No political-economic system of any great worth has ever survived successfully (to the benefit of the general populace), without virtue in the people and in their leadership. Virtue is defined as behavior showing high moral standards. It is "the" essential element for a civil society. However, in our present-day American society, the function of being "politically correct"...is to hide the public from incriminating behaviors or unpleasant realities...the opposite of virtuous behavior. In politics it is a clever way to divert attention from issues that should be directly addressed, in order that a politician may remain popular and retain job security in a powerful and lucrative position. Allowing this will be our ultimate demise. If traditional America is to survive, we must realize we are at the crossroads of keeping our Christian virtue and our inspired Constitution.

While other books on this subject attack socialism by using character assassination of those who contributed to its rise during the early industrial revolution, this book ignores these involved personal profiles, even if the criticisms are justified. There is no need for extensive personal attacks to explain why socialism is inherently dysfunctional to humans...regardless of whatever permutations individuals attempt to make of it. Logic and historical example is mostly sufficient. This book explains why *virtue* is inherent in capitalism and social programs, and why it is not inherent in corporatism or socialism. Other books also focus on the dysfunction and failure of socialism rather than the successful function of capitalism. Both are explained in contrast and in relation to each other in this book.

Finally, other books, while more scholarly, are so involved in saying similar things in many sophisticated ways, they become a sleep aid. Most people are simply not going to buy or read them because of this complexity. This book helps the typical reader to grasp the rudiments to guide them in understanding the more complex. I try not to say something more than once, unless a connection or point is emphasized. Key word meaning is ferreted out for definition, from which to make a coherent argument. Without agreement in word meaning, there is little ground for understanding, and no point in arguing. Confusion on word meaning is a diversionary tactic employed by those who wish to remain in denial. They are free to do so.

As an example of clarity in definition, I could compare communism and socialism. Communism is a political control structure superimposed on the economics of socialism. Socialism's meaning is the collective ownership in the economic factors of production. With the meanings clear, we can explain that through centralization, the economics of socialism lends itself well to the political authoritarianism and autocracy of communism. With these definitions in agreement, I can explain how socialism prepares itself, by its very nature, to be controlled by an individual or group that seeks power over all others. I give some fundamental explanations of how it happens. Brief examples are (1) a society seeking a path of least resistance through collectivism and centralization, (2) narcissistic personalities who crave power and control over others, and (3) a desire by passive-dependent oriented personalities for caretakers (for which narcissistic personalities are happy to oblige). These and other elements come together to form a collective dysfunctional codependency that is inherent in socialism, and which is dangerous to individual independence, and ultimately, a healthy and economically viable society.

I examine the modern origin and nature of capitalism, social programs, corporatism and socialism. Socialism and corporatism are explained in relation to pertinent concepts such as modern liberalism and extremism. The best way to examine something you intend to criticize...is to focus first on the best arguments for it, rather than against it. Objectivity is better accomplished this way. I expand throughout the book on the importance of *virtue* in the various constructs of American society. Social extremisms and their origins are examined and explained in relation to politics, science, religion, law, and other areas. Geniuses, scholars, experts, intellectuals and doctoral professors all condescend to layman's language to explain their ideas to the general public. I am none of these. Layman's language is the only one I know. Condescension will be unnecessary. (For the reader's convenience all citations are in the general text. *A source, bibliographic reference number, and the year of the source* are included.)

Introduction

From ancient prophets and philosophers to modern-day sociologists, people have theorized on what constitutes "The Good Life". Such prominent people in the past have associated the good life with virtue. However, in modern times, others associate the good life with material wealth and prestige. Few argue that wealth can bring temporary happiness and relief, but in time, many find out (often the hard way), it is not the key to the good life. This is not to say in any manner that poverty is preferable to wealth. It is not. All need adequate providence of sustenance. However, whether one is rich or poor, I believe virtue adds in abundant measure to the good life of the individual. This book addresses two "isms" which actually have more in common than is generally realized, corporatism and socialism. Both seek an assurance in economic security through the control of others, without regard to personal merit, liberty, faith, or virtue. Both lead to society-wide tragedies.

Many today question the idea of putting the word "American" next to the word "virtue". Synonyms for virtue are goodness, righteousness, morality, integrity, dignity, rectitude, honor, decency, respectability, nobility, worthiness, and purity. Daily acts of virtue by good people are as countless as the stars. However, when certain public figures avoid addressing virtue...particularly their own...there ought to be great concern about that person. Political, media, entertainment, and corporate leaders are often corrupted by power, fame, lusts and money. Corruption has always existed in large societies. In 21st century America, *Corporatism* has become a powerful source of corruption. The definition for corporatism I use in this book is "the control of a state *[legislature]* or organization by large interest groups". (*Google search*) Today, that large interest group in particular, is the *financial sector*. There is a critically imminent concern about the degree and scope of this corruption. We are seeing, almost monthly, the worsening effect it has on society.

People err and break laws that affect society...so they attempt to remedy those mistakes through governance, legislation, and enforcement. Many secularists believe corruption is a function of social dysphoria and disorganization. I disagree. I believe it is a function of the individual not choosing to be virtuous. Many so-called progressives say we must *change* our Constitution and our values to align with the "modern world". This would be a grave mistake. What sort of government is best? I will make the case for traditional America. I refer collectively to its constitution, form of government, and economic system. I believe the U.S. Constitution is the most inspired document ever created for the governance of a large populace. Our *Constitution*...working alongside *Federalism* and *Capitalism*...presents to the world no better existing governing system and economy for a virtuous...yet imperfect...people.

America is now at crossroads. Are Americans willing to maintain their virtue? *Socialism*, posing in its various forms, is in resurgence among our youth. They have not experienced what former generations have. Modern life has sheltered many of them from the harsh psychological and physical realities of a more primitive existence. There are many permutations of applied and ideological socialism. To address its core problems, I stick strictly to the economic definition. *Socialism is a theory or system of social organization in which the means of production and distribution of goods are owned and controlled either collectively or by the government.* The modern economic collectivism of socialism is geared to a so-called practical *distribution*...derived from a subjective evaluation of *contribution*. In applying this artificially contrived system, it insidiously seeks to circumvent the natural consequences of choice, faith, merit, and virtue in economic activity.

However, our security, along with liberty, personal merit, and risks...is cradled in *virtue*...not a subjective *pragmatics*. It is for this reason the American system is antagonistic towards socialism, dictatorship, modern globalism, social extremism, fundamentalism, corporatism, etc...all which lead to bad governance and the eventual loss of faith, liberty, and virtue. People today often confuse the various social programs that capitalism funds through taxation with socialism. This is due to a confusion in definition. The source of most government taxation that funds effective social programs is from privately owned, rather than public or government owned production (production meaning goods and services). Agreement in word definition is critical. If we are to fix the harm we are doing to a nation of youth being misled by modern academia, media, and politics...the ideas in this book are essential for them to understand.

Before proceeding further, I ask the question...what it is it about socialism that appeals to people, such that even after all the recent historic failures...like the Soviet Union, Albania, Venezuela, North Korea, and so on...that they continue to reconsider it from generation to generation? Socialism is a "feel good" concept. Imagining its success might be comforting, but it has always remained incomplete as a "blood and guts" functioning system. Like the late Rodney King, we might ask... "why can't we all just get along?". We know the answer...but we hide it from ourselves to maintain a pleasant illusion. We like the idea of being free from having to responsibly insure providence for ourselves...hoping that someone else will take care of us. Another "pitfall" is the catharsis of *victimhood* that socialism encourages. Feeling sorry for ourselves assages our guilt due to envy and personal inaction. Wallowing in self-pity means we can escape feeling responsible for ourselves, and blame someone or something else for an undesirable condition or situation. Yes, there are people who do terrible things…but it's not an excuse to escape struggles or to stop trying.

If one has ever taken the time to read up on the various works promoting socialism, a common thread you might pick up from many of the authors, is their apparent perpetual discontent with present society. Whether that is actually a reflection of personal discontent, I don't know. There seems to be a condition that permeates the life of a hard-core socialist. It is a desire to seek change in the superstructures of society as opposed to considering change within oneself. It is as if one believes changing the environment will magically change and satisfy oneself, circumventing personal character development considerations. Self-improvement to getting a better job or relationship is not an answer, because they decide they are "fine" the way they are…their efforts are enough. It's always the system that's at fault, never themselves.

This attitude colors their perspective on history and events, as they use (waste?) their time in writing and arguing historical revisions they feel will justify their poor choices. Socialism never dies because there are always those who choose to succumb to its false, empty, and lethal sirens. It is the endless pursuit of a collective utopia devoid of merit, liberty and faith. In formulating their new world, freedom and free will of individuals is always discarded as a means to their desired end result. Socialism is the ultimate philosophy in assuring that one will maintain these self-defeating behaviors. I don't mean to characterize all socialists as being this way, but the general philosophy itself is dangerous in that it leads to this perspective.

Chapter 1

American Governance

Psychology and Government

The lust for power, control, and other prevalent weaknesses...seems inherent in human beings possessing free will. Such flaws within us make good governance for a large populace nearly impossible to achieve. The closest we have come for a sizable population in the modern era...is the confluence of the U.S. Constitution, Federalism, and Capitalism. While our Constitution presents us a *just and merciful* "rule of law" to preserve our freedoms, Federalism seeks to insure a "separation" and a "balance" of powers between the major branches of our government (executive, legislative, judicial), and between the levels of government (federal and state). (*Vocabulary.com, 1, undated*) Working in concert to preserve our freedoms is capitalism, with its incentives for opportunity and possession.

As long as these branches and levels of governance maintain mutual antagonisms in supporting the rule of law...and the incentives of opportunity and possession provide a fair competitiveness...this has proven to be the best way to keep the tyrannical tendencies of individuals and groups from destroying the freedoms and opportunities of the whole. Sadly, when certain people get a little authority, it is in their nature to abuse it to control others. This is why our constitution and government will keep different powers divided up among different authorities…and to have in place the policies and procedures that will protect individual freedoms for expression, desire, and action.

The genius of the U.S. Constitution is its realization and consideration of human frailty and the unstable moral dynamics of our imperfect souls. This imperfection in human psychology is conceptually inherent in the Christian doctrine that "no man is without sin" and ALL are in need of humble repentance. (*Romans 5:12-13*) Knowing our nature with gaining power, it is therefore reasoned, power is best separated among various groups with different purposes, and with different understandings. A separation of powers permits a "watchdog" co-surveillance to prevail between the various branches and levels of government, keeping them in check. This, in turn, allows for the continued existence of *pluralism*…which is crucial for the protection of the rights of the majority, the minority, and for each individual.

Pluralism is defined as "a state of society in which members of diverse ethnic, racial, religious, or social groups maintain and develop their traditional cultures or special interests within the confines of a common civilization." (*Wikipedia, 2, 2017*) We shouldn't take for granted the inspired nature of our constitution, form of government, and the freedoms, rights, and protections, to allow for the pursuit of each individual's unique sense of happiness. Through this system a far greater percentage in the nation's population has achieved a standard of living that provides for a remarkable quality of life, surpassing, by the numbers…any in history.

Documents of our Virtue

A good standard of living does not necessarily guarantee a high quality of life or happiness. I believe virtue is crucial to this result. Yet, this virtue and its derivative values and ethics...must come from some divine source...for without this source, there exists no true morality, and therefore, no way to define it. It is anyone's guess or preference, collectively or otherwise. The United States Constitution is illuminated by the principles set forth in the Declaration of Independence, which states..."We hold these truths to be self-evident". How can moral truths be self-evident? There must exist, a "higher law"...[an absolute] of right and wrong...from which to derive human law. This is manifest in human conscience. It is, therefore, not political will...but rather our moral reasoning...that is the foundation of our constitution and system.

It thus follows..."the cardinal moral truths are these: That all Men are created equal, that they are endowed by their Creator with certain unalienable Rights, that among these are Life, Liberty, and the Pursuit of Happiness...That to secure these Rights, Governments are instituted among Men, deriving their just Powers from the Consent of the Governed" *(Declaration of Independence - Cato Institute, 3, 1998)*. The majority of the "governed" in America believe in God, and it is through this source of absolute morality...that right and wrong exist...not in a vague or relative sense. It is by this belief in a pure morality that we are effectively self-governed.

Our Constitution, thus being derived from the morality of our Declaration...along with its implication of inherent free will in each individual...means America's moral foundation for freedom and choice is distinctly Biblical, and therefore, Judeo-Christian. Aside from a few anomalies such as Thomas Moore, the Founders of America were predominantly Christian...meaning...they believed in Biblically derived concepts such as the sovereign authority of God, absolute morality, rule of law, restitution, liberty, equality, family, free enterprise, private property, a fair trial, and so forth. *(Britannica, 4, Online)* Most of all, we believe in virtue. While it would take time before events such as the *civil rights movement* and *equal rights for women* to take form, the U.S. Constitution laid the foundation from which these social changes would spawn, preserve, and prevail.

Freedom Leads to Wealth

Only a free society with the challenges of liberty and risk, can accommodate the uniqueness and the inherent rights of individuals. There are many who would sacrifice liberty in favor of a less complicated centralized economy and governance such as socialism. This mindset portends a dangerous and false sense of security. A naive utopian vision and hope of a simplistic "Walden Pond" world is not enough to make it so. *(Thoreau, 5, 1843)* Such a world can only exist by a purer virtue within a collective populace. The ideal itself is not the problem. People are the problem.

A declaration of independence by Americans was made to England and its monarchy. To achieve broad freedoms, it would be necessary to implement a new constitution recognizing an extension of the separation of powers. This would also lead to an expanded pluralism in eventually creating and preserving greater personal liberties for all. Following the Revolutionary War, Americans with inspired constitutional documentation and new freedoms expanded the work on free market capitalism. Contrary to popular belief, free markets are not as haphazard as one might think.

The formula for generating material wealth for the masses is (1) granting the right of private ownership of property, (2) capital, or the machinery, buildings, and fiscal operations to produce products or services, (3) a labor source, or industrious human capital, (4) knowledge, meaning the possession of proprietary information and intellectual capital through research, innovation, invention, discovery, and development... and finally (5) entrepreneurs, or those individuals with the personal characteristics to withstand the pressures of high risk and failure, which enable them to make use of the aforementioned. (*Knudsen, Swedburg, 6, 2009*)

It is estimated by some economists that only about 5% of the population have the personal "wherewithal" to be highly successful entrepreneurs. (*fitsmallbusiness.com, 7, 2019*) Nevertheless, it is this 5% that makes the rest of America, including the poor and middle-class, much richer. Only a land that provides broad freedoms can create the right atmosphere and conditions in which the masses can enjoy great wealth. Even many of those meeting the poverty index in America today seem to live as kings (compared to the dark ages, and to the view of present third or second world countries). America is special in this respect and the reason they were the envy of the 20th Century. Other nations took note to their own benefit.

A transcendent confluence in Christian cannon, Greek polity, Roman legality, British parliamentary procedure, etc., resulted in the development of the principles underpinning the Declaration of Independence. Eleven years later, following a war, came the U.S. Constitution... then its Bill of Rights. James Madison formulated the Bill of Rights (the first ten amendments) to protect the individual rights of minorities (in particular the rich of that day) from being trampled by the democratic majority. However, this works in favor of the poor and middle-class as well. (*The Politics Book, 8, 2013*) It is this principle of fair representation of minorities that is inherent the *electoral college*. This, along with Federalisms' separation of powers, would help to insure the new nation extensive checks and balances...against inevitable political corruption, illegal successions, power monopolies, and mob or military coups...through a constitutional democratic republic. (*The Federalist Papers [10], 9, 1786-1800*)

The idea of a "melting pot" was meant to be inclusive and tolerant (at least as most interpret it today) not only of differences in race, nationality, or religion, but also in governing. This pluralism along with new freedoms led to a remarkable series of events unlike any recorded in history. A convergence of talented, industrious, and inspired people, along with world changing events...a continuing renaissance of the arts and sciences, enlightened economic theory, technological development, scientific discovery, unprecedented religious reformations and extended freedoms...forged a nation of immigrants from the four corners of the earth, that emerged with a stunning rate of progress to create the most powerful nation ever.

Explorers, scientists, engineers, builders, farmers, teachers, entrepreneurs, venture capitalists, architects, inventors and others discovered and created great wealth. Wealth is gained by enterprise, innovation, healthy competition, private land ownership, the availability of labor, harvesting natural resources, banking and other activities and conditions. Wealth is also made possible by breathing the air, drinking water, and eating from the various seeds of growth provided by creation. One would think a wealthy person of good fortune would be grateful and willing to help others. The innumerable charitable foundations established is evidence of this.

Economic Policy and Criminality

What of the dishonorable? Naturally, wise and just regulation is essential to a healthy market economy. A careful use of *Keynesian* (measured intervention) economics, within *Laissez Faire* (natural course) economics and U.S. economic policy should foster a continued expansion of the middle-class through the ongoing enfranchisement of the poorer class...without encouraging criminal or unethical conduct. Is this process and progress spotless? Hardly. Nevertheless, a propagation and broad flow of free markets is something that classical capitalism accomplishes that socialism, for example, cannot. Government, however, can also work against this propagation and flow by over-burdening tax-payers with costly artificial programs, and imposing stifling regulation based on misguided bias and conjecture. This circumvents natural market and business processes that could otherwise, permanently boost jobs and the economy.

In addition, those who ignore the national debt and the impact of a yearly budget deficit on this debt, fail to see...or are indifferent to...what constitutes true wealth. A government creating and distributing vapid forms of currency or credit without product (goods and services) representation is never a viable economic strategy. Very generally speaking, most currency is neither a service nor a good. It's basically a pricing mechanism for exchange. Most currency has no intrinsic value except as an abstract agreement in the form of coin, paper, or digital stream...that allows common transactional commerce (to access services and goods) across vast expanses of population and geography. It is a tool of distribution within cooperating markets. Without actual products underpinning that currency, it becomes worthless.

Currency, therefore, increases or decreases in value depending on the effects of several economic variables related to products...such as supply and demand...and even faith. It's ultimate value, however, is based on developed goods and services (existing resources). People can create as much wealth as they desire, but it requires certain types of efforts, co-operation, timeliness, accessibility, labor, and ideation...in correlation with the raw materials and energies of the earth. Currency loses value when it fails to reflect or represent the goods and services that actually exist in a marketplace. Questionable financial instruments and strategies can easily distort and confuse a true reflection. This will, in time, create false economic bubbles or vapid markets that foster unethical and criminal activities, with markets eventually collapsing.

Consumers vs. State

Value is subject to a population. Consumers determine what is of value to society. "Valued" needs and wants are fluid and ever changing. Yet, this value determines what is produced for profit. Pre-calculating these ever-changing subjective values every day for millions is impossible. Information for production comes every day to thousands of industries, and from every demographic of the consumers. The supply and demand of products determines value, and therefore price. *Price signals*, for example, are used to determine the type and amount of material and labor for the effective, and therefore profitable, production of goods and services. To suggest that a government determine what is of value to people, and what products are made, is ludicrous, unprofitable, and ultimately destructive.

Millions of consumers provide information daily that a nationalized government could never mentally process. However, growth in productivity is essential to a healthy economy and society. Market prices provide feedback on what sells and how much. It tells industries how to adjust. Socialism stifles production growth (Gross National Product and Gross Domestic Product) because the means of production is centralised, collectivised, and determined by a few, such that information from price signals no longer exist. Millions of consumers are not allowed to determine what their needs or wants are, and therefore, what is produced. The industries relying on getting or using that information are also lost. Division of labor is diminished and, therefore, the millions of specialized jobs created by it. Consumers must always determine what is produced, not the State.

Price signals to consumers and producers are foundational to effective economics. "Price signals communicate in such a way that prevents massive shortages and surpluses and ensures that consumer wants are largely satisfied. The actual price of a good or a service - in this case - gasoline, provides an incentive to buyers and sellers. For example, after a natural disaster, the supply disruption would cause the price of gasoline to rise. Just as a traffic light sends signals to drivers coming from many directions, allowing for a smooth flow of traffic, higher gasoline prices would signal to buyers to reduce their consumption and to sellers to increase their production. And both would have an incentive to do so. In this way, price signals allow markets to function efficiently under many kinds of conditions." (*St. Louis Federal - Podcast, 10, undated*)

Price signals can't be replicated by pre-forecasting. The reason is because the signals change daily according to millions of consumer's needs and wants. Price signals are a mass-psychological phenomenon, and subjective in nature. Because they can't be forecasted beyond the immediacy by sheer numbers and spread, pre-planning the economy is not possible. The Soviet Union and others found this out about nationalized socialism the brutally hard way. This is one primary reason why nationalizing and centralizing industries in an economy of millions always fails.

Another common misconception regarding economics is that the world has scarce *raw materials*. A companion fallacy regarding economics is that wealth is finite and fixed…that if one person gets 15 percent of something, then that leaves only 85 percent for the rest of us. In practical reality this is false. One cannot define wealth in this context. Wealth is the ideation in people using raw materials and energy to create new products and services that people want or need. Agricultural scientists know, for example, that we produce enough food right now to feed the world 1 1/2 times over. (*Gimenez, 11, 2014*)

The reason it doesn't get used right…beyond criminal and wartime confiscations…is due to psychological barriers of fear and distrust, disagreements within politics, values and ideologies that negatively affect resource acquisition/distribution, people not uniting or unionizing for moral change, and the constraints of socio-political geographic boundaries. These man-made barriers are what create pockets of *scarce resources*. The earth and humans, in general, do not have scarce materials or ideation. True capitalism doesn't try to control people's economic or personal values. Socialism seeks to control material and spiritual values, because that is the only way they can get it to work...yet it doesn't...because it goes against human nature.

Decentralization vs. Centralization

Regarding Federalism...the U.S. federal government, individual states and Native American reservations have a unique tripartite plenary (complete in itself) system. This decentralized multi-sovereignty lends definition and fiber to the nation's economic and socio-political infrastructure...including a heightened commercial efficiency in natural and industrial resource acquisition, maintenance, and distribution. When the federal government tries to "centralize" functions beyond its principle duties of national security and basic national regulation, it unnecessarily creates...as a matter of course...perpetual bureaucracy and red tape for each of the states.

This overreach can destroy efficiencies and self-reliances that otherwise only the individual states can effectively address according to their respective population, geography, climate, natural resources and other characteristics unique to each state. When states and reservations are individually strong, so is the nation. However, at the federal level, the effects of geographical distance and demographics is often ignored...as timely controls in real-world processes and practical resolutions to on-sight realities are overlooked or dismissed. Misapplied centralization is an example of bad government. Finding a balance is crucial.

A guarantee of opportunity…not success

There are those who feel everyone should be equal, financially and otherwise, regardless of merit or personal desires. The Constitution of the United States does not say this. It does imply (as interpreted by most people today) that all people are *equal* as humans. It also implies that all people should have the freedom to pursue their dreams. By extension we should understand everyone should be given fair or equal opportunity to achieve his or her aspirations. A so-called new democratic socialism suggest a centralized economic collective in which all are given according to contribution…but who is to decide the definition and values of contribution? Is there a special listing for this? Is there an omnipotent individual or group on earth that knows this?

There are no guarantees here, nor should there be. There are natural forces far beyond the control of either government or economy. People must "earn" their own happiness by whatever honorable means that may entail. That may not always mean financial wealth. Everyone has a different idea of what kind of success may bring him or her happiness. It is paramount that our government ensures people have their freedom to pursue happiness, but without attempting to define individual success or guaranteeing anyone anything. Nobel Laureate Milton Friedman queries…"Is then the search for fairness all a mistake? Not at all. There is a real role for fairness, but that role is in constructing general rules and adjudicating disputes about the rules, not in determining the outcome of our separate activities." (*Friedman, 12, 1977*)

Unfortunately, it must also be stated…there is an undercurrent within the ethos of the American business community that greed is an essential element to succeed. Ambition may be, but greed ultimately destroys. Some have confused the greed of corporatism with the ambition of capitalism. Corporatism happens when government becomes unethically involved with influencing big business. Elitists can influence legislation through corrupt politicians, to favor policy that gives certain corporations unfair advantage in the marketplace, often leading to what is called *financialization* (illegal transactions, monopolies, offshoring, bailouts, and other destructive market influences). This actually does great damage to classic capitalism. Regulators are expected to catch such activities and prosecute the players. Unfortunately, the regulators themselves may be corrupt. An illegal corporate strategy is to get a regulator on their side (regulation capture). This is why virtue is so essential in those we put in office...and should impact our personal decisions as to which services and people we choose in doing our personal business.

Collectivism...It Doesn't Work

Kristian Niemietz states that ideas are better when the results are ignored. (*Niemietz, 13, 2019*) This is true of collectivism. Collectivism is the central philosophical component of socialism. Niemietz uses the idea of a raindance to bring rain. It goes something like this...if the raindance fails...then it was never a raindance. If socialism fails...then it was never socialism. This is the excuse given by those who championed it, then observed only failure and tragedy. Collectivism is defined as the practice or principle of giving a group priority over each individual in it. While this may work well for ants or bees...it should never be applied as a general principle to humans. Despite the objections of some offended environmental extremists, we are infinitely more complex than insects. Anyone who wants to try collectivism without the consideration of an impossible coalescence in all humans, good luck to you. Let me save you the trouble...it won't work, and you will create more war trying.

Democratic Socialism is a myth and a contradiction. Democracy refers to the political representation of the majority. The majority are free as individuals to vote for whatever people and social issues they want. Democracy does not mean people will vote as a group, but rather independently. It is, therefore, not a collective. On the other hand, Socialism is when the means of production of goods and services is publicly owned by a collective, meaning "the people", or the government. However, it is impossible for a collective of millions to own and control an industry and regulate its production. How would 350 million individuals, or even thousands of government workers, for that matter... own, cooperate, and make decisions about a corporation that makes a particular line of cars? Would each individual have a say in the various thousands of parts, coming from many other industries that create those various parts, before a car is put together? How would you organize a meeting for such a mass of people for daily or hourly decision making?

In reality Democratic Socialism is a nonsensical term. The two words, democracy and socialism, are in opposition. When a country's government is given control of expanding social programs to be distributed to the people made affordable by the taxation of private industries, that is the definition of capitalism, not socialism. In addition, charities, fundraisers, foundations, and other service entities, are also far more likely to be developed along with government social programs under capitalism. Socialism results in the opposite...the eventual demise of these social programs and entities. The key to a viable economy and social programs is preserving capitalism, rather than desperately resorting to socialism. To preserve capitalism is to address the pertinent issues of corruption from corporatism, the misguided or neglected economic education in our schools and universities, and to emphasize the importance of virtue in our society. These are the actions that will prevent the destruction of our economy and our society.

Chapter 2

The U.S. Constitution: A Standard for the World

Church and State

A Constitutional issue often abused is separation of Church and State. To the founding fathers, the First Amendment existed to keep the state out of the church...not the church out of the state. This means religion is not to be silenced by the government in the public sphere. The phrase "separation of church and state" doesn't occur anywhere in the Constitution. It is a phrase invented in an attempt to explain the First Amendment: "Congress shall make no law respecting an establishment of religion, or prohibiting the free exercise thereof". (*Zachary Lee, 14, 2013*) Lee explains that this is the extent of this passage from the First Amendment.

An instance of a government controlled by a church (specific religion) was The Church of England. British taxation was controlled by this theocratic body. The Founding Fathers of America were against having a "government" church...as it violated the principle behind freedom of religion...meaning everyone's religion is respected. However, there is nowhere in the U.S. Constitution that forbids individuals from mixing faith and politics, or from sharing their faith (including millinialisms, atheisms, deisms, humanisms, and other isms) in a state-related function or location. The historical facts show that no one interpreted the First Amendment to exclude religion from the political sphere. Some examples Lee uses are: The U.S. Congress used to hold Christian worship services at the Capitol on Sundays. The Supreme Court Building was used to house church services on Sundays.

Lee continues...Twelve of the original 14 states required religious tests for those seeking public office. After the Civil War, the First Congregational Church of Washington used the House of Representatives as a worship building. In 1863, the U.S. Senate requested that Abraham Lincoln designate an official day of national prayer and humility. In 1944, Franklin D. Roosevelt (as well as presidents before him) went on radio and prayed nationally for our troops and our nation. (I note here that more recently in 2017, the Republican Legislature decided to hold regular Bible studies on Capitol Hill).

UN Law vs. the U.S. Constitution

The United Nations is a voluntary cooperative governing body. It's main objective is to prevent war. It is not a nation of people. It has no land. It has little assets beyond some building usage and nations agreeing to give it money. It is able...through charitable donations...to fund a small military, various humanitarian units, and travel to meeting places to reach agreements to assist the oppressed. (*Wikipedia UN, 15, undated*) That it's agenda could even approach governing an actual nation, let alone over 220 plus nations and territories, is fallacious thinking. In response to its so-called globalist agenda...it is incumbent upon Americans to help the international community understand...it is the ideals and structure of the U.S. Constitution that should be considered in the development and application of UN Law, and not the other way around. However, because the U.S. Constitution is of an inspired nature...it requires the "virtue" of the people.

The question that should be asked is...are the countries of the world ready for the responsibilities inherent in these rights that lead to great individual opportunity and personal liberty? Some have achieved much already, and some are ready to...but many are not. It is disingenuous and antithetical to impose American representative democracy on a society that doesn't want it, or is not ready for it. Those peoples and personalities that succumb to laziness, oppression, fear and tyranny... without the virtue, sacrifice, work-ethic, mental constitution, personal disposition and willingness to fight for these rights and freedoms... would quickly lose such a constitution and the civilization it is founded on. A virtuous leadership and populace is required for a constitutional democratic republic.

Lesser governments, such as dictatorships, lead to tyranny. Regarding these narcissistic, control-craved tyrants...it is impossible for them to see other people as little more than animated objects to be suppressed and oppressed for their own purposes. Only they and their ideas are important...other individuals are not. They don't see people as complex social-emotional beings of great individual worth. They can't comprehend that most of us will never deny our own rights to think, feel, express and act upon the world as independent agents. Yet, good people realize we do not live alone and just for ourselves. Good people understand that with personal agency comes responsibility and consequence. To allow for everyone's freedoms as much as possible, we agree to fundamental underlying values, ethics, and rules that permit everyone as much freedom as possible...without infringing upon the rights and responsibilities of others. This results in a pluralism that the U.S. Constitution best achieves...but only through our virtue.

The U.S. Constitution vs. Sharia

The purely religious aspects of a traditional moderate Islam can peacefully coexist in America...but only under the rule and protection of the

U.S. Constitution. If *radical* Islam's intent is to take over America from within...through subterfuge and deception...then this constitutes sedition and must be dealt with. I use the word "radical" to distinguish it from...and to protect...traditional Islam. Concerning today's radical elements, it is not in God's purpose or disposition, as general Christianity understands it...to force truth (as assumed or otherwise) on anyone. Additionally, revenge is never justified under any circumstance. All Americans are expected to understand there are personal, natural, spiritual, and/or social and legal consequences for breaking American law...in which both *justice and mercy* are inextricably bound in the concept of "no cruel and unusual punishment".

Sharia is considered inseparable from modern Islam by tens of millions of those of the more contemporary fundamentalist persuasions. It is also meant to be a constitution of political, religious, legal, educational, and military applications based on Islamic principles...just as the U.S. Constitution is based on Judeo-Christian principles. One cannot serve two masters. These disparate constitutions are critically at odds due to very different values and views of freedom and free will...inherent in...and germane to...the U.S. Constitution. The U.S. Constitution and Sharia cannot politically coexist in the real world. While Muslims of moderate persuasions may be agreeable to this realization...yet worldwide...neo-Islam often encapsulates a more dogmatic thinking incompatible with America. Traditional America never imposes religion on others.

One can never justify imposing one's will upon another...rationalizing it as "God's will" or a claim of "superior wisdom". Sharia is "Islamic canonical law based on the teachings of the Koran and the traditions of the Prophet (Hadith and Sunna), prescribing both religious *and* secular duties..." (*Google Dictionary, 16, Sharia*). World-wide Sharia interpretations are most often indifferent to personal liberty...as is socialism. The similarity between an enforced theocratic one-world-order and an enforced socialistic one-world-order (whether directly imposed or achieved by subterfuge), comes down to *control* over the individual. If Muslims wish to integrate into the pluralism of American society, the essential concepts of spirituality they must learn are liberty and free will of the Individual. Would not this be Allah's (God's) will?

A Flawed World Agenda

Few people question that the goal of the United Nations is a one-world order based on a unidimensionally structured socialism. Pluralism is at odds with this unidimensional world socialism. Ultimately, it denies the liberties of disparate personalities, with variable innate beliefs and ambitions. Social-economic collectivists ignore the complexity of the individual...i.e., the social-psychology of an imperfect, ever-changing human being...living within a complex ecology and economy. Socialism is naturally hegemonic and is, therefore, allergic to the discipline and character requirements of the individual in adapting to a pluralistic, merit-based society. Further, it does not comprehend that *rationing* never achieves "according to need", and therefore, any semblance of "fairness" is never the result. (*Agenda 21, 17, 2019*)

Under Socialism, the resources distributed by a world council would be owned by the controlling government...or the people collectively (the same difference when considering that some person or group will be in control of this "collective resource"). Consider this analogy from Pearl Harbor. Before the U.S. got involved directly in WWII, an officer in charge decided to organize all our combat planes all in one place...to make storage and order easier. When Japan attacked...it easily identified and destroyed most of our planes in a single attack. The same is true of socialism and its authoritarian centralized simplification. All that would need to happen for catastrophic failure...because everyone is under a collective resource...is to permit a single individual, or a group of individuals...in control...such as would start to act as a dictator or a tyrannical council. When the people controlled by the UN council have an opinion and the controller(s) disagree, they will start to decide what is right and wrong for those people who have become dependent on their resources.

The ideology of socialism is a ruse and a snare based on wishful thinking. Yet, in its absolute sovereignty...there exists no viable balance of powers for a deterrent. One should understand that UBI (Unconditional/Universal Basic Income) promoted by the United Nations is incipient socialism. Whether a tyrannical leadership is atheistic or religious in nature will not matter. Protocols for identification...such as used in fascist Nazi Germany are inevitable. For the controllers, the end will justify the means. It will be analogous to (if not fulfillment of) the Christian prophecy in Revelation...only those with a certain [digital-based?] "mark" of sorts on their body,,,will be given resources. (*Revelation 14:9, 11*) Those who disagree...or perhaps refuse to deny a supernal being or savior...will be left to themselves, possibly even destroyed for treason against the new world order. Some people also forget the supremacist Nazis (who murdered millions), were National Socialists, a form of race-based socialism. Yet, very few socialists and liberal politicians really understand the complex social-psychological and economic mechanisms behind a capitalistic free market system. I believe those who do...and continue to pursue such a simplistic economic ideology as socialism...should question their own morality.

Capitalism vs. Corporatism

Socialists often point their finger at corrupt individuals in high places, ignoring their own logical fallacies and hypocrisies, in attacking capitalism out of context. For example, monopolies that are created dishonestly by the shared special interests of government, corporations, or elitists is the definition of corporatism. It has nothing to do with capitalism. Corporatism is merely another form of corruption. It is anti-capitalist, anti-competition, illegal and destructive. (*Urban Diction-ary, 18, 2010*) True capitalism is in *how* we work...with personal integrity...whether by working hard, flexibly, smartly, honestly, freely, etc,... not by greed through deception.

Laissez-faire economics best relates to Adam Smith's idea of the *invisible hand.* (*Smith, 19, 1776*) The more modern concept is that, left to chance and opportunity...and by having certain characteristics of industry, fair competition, ambition (defined as a healthy socio-biological motivation to achieve a good quality of life for self and others), innovation and motivation towards self-preservation, and respect for freedoms...people will take care of others best by first (morally and responsibly) taking care of their own interests (self and family) in personal finance, health, education, etc. Alexis de Tocqueville introduced this as the philosophy of *enlightened self-interest.* (*Tocqueville, 20, 1835*)

The invisible hand (the reciprocating virtues of goodwill and effort) is something that benefits everyone. In this manner we put ourselves in a position to help others. One can have natural self-interests and simultaneously others interests at heart. In classic capitalism, there is no implied contradiction between oneself and others welfare. When addressing corruption, the mitigation of criminal influence to manageable levels is accomplished by a strong private sector...in which business creation and development is fostered through modern banking practices...which review and structure business plans, and loan currency to small businesses, which may or may not become large corporations. This creates job hiring on a massive scale, with another bonus being, less people opting for criminal lifestyles to survive.

One should be able to comprehend that one cannot artificially impose wage amounts, when the success of each business is contingent on a unique business model, that contours itself to a free market in a specific demographic. These businesses that hire for private sector jobs provide revenue through taxation to the local, state, and federal governing bodies to provide more public sector jobs in utilities, policing, fire stations, regulation, and national security. One can easily extrapolate that from the activities of the private sector, come more jobs for the public sector, as well as, the means to protect our homes, schools, and churches with powerful military and policing forces controlled by the people, for the people, through the rule of law. For socialists to maintain that classic capitalism creates injustices is demonstrative of a particular ignorance in definition, as well as, cause and effect.

A modern pathological work culture

There is an existential utopian argument that when an individual has the benefit of good genes and a good environment, then that individual will be good. One problem with this thinking is that we have innumerable case histories in military, criminal, and domestic life that demonstrate otherwise. If good genes and a privileged upbringing guarantee good people, then why is there so much evidence to the contrary? In any case, we should acknowledge unethical and criminal behavior. There are disgruntled workers, desensitized business people, and white-collar embezzlers in the financial sector who think of the world as a godless playground.

Some pathological "go-getters" consider those who are unwilling to compromise their principles for personal gain, as naïve people...destined for a dreary existence without fun and pleasure. They may feel others who do not seek the things they seek are fools and losers. These extreme perspectives have become part of a corrupt code of ethics in various corporate and political arenas, including the small-business world. Some of them assume anyone stupid enough not to go along with them deserves to be taken advantage of.

Peer pressure is extreme under a severe and subversive work-culture philosophy of greed, that if you want a job in a particular firm or industry that pays, you must conform to that culture and the behaviors that enable fast quarterly profits and advancement over others so that not only are the stockholders and other shareholders happy, but there is plenty left over for extravagant bonuses, huge raises, and lavish perks for the so-called "winners". For these people...charitable donations are only given for good public relations and tax breaks.

The leaders of such entities are often the type of people who laugh at the poor and have plenty of funds to lobby those politicians who are either corrupt, or naïve enough to believe there are good intentions behind all corporate welfare. The game of playing good workers against each other in the very same organization seems a form of sadistic amusement for the elite. Some of the wealthy also acquire greater wealth through shady stock practices, backroom financial schemes, illegal connections, insider trading, brutal in-house...hyper-competitive personnel policy, etc. at the expense of many jobs, individual loss, and a sicker workforce.

If the middle-class becomes perpetually weakened by this greed and arrogance, it also puts our national security at risk. Other countries will move in with their own capital and gradually eat away at the infrastructure of our economy, our freedoms, and eventually, our way of life. Many greedy people cannot help themselves. Like gambling and other addictions, one should realize, those pathologically addicted to accumulating and/or wasting vast wealth, need serious psychological help. For the addict, people become secondary to the addiction. Will we succumb to the comforts and conveniences of the present at the expense of the future? Virtue and vigilance must be emphasized in all our economic classes for high schools and colleges. It will lead to higher ethics and a better understanding of the role of Capitalism within our Constitution.

Chapter 3

Globalism's Ultimate Failure

Economic Philosophy 101

The freedom to risk, to own, to innovate...are all crucial to human motivation and progress. America is a constitutional (rule of law), democratic (by the people), republic (through fair representation). Our constitutional democratic republic is run by a free market economy with an emphasis on classic capitalism. Although social programs are implemented by government, this is not the same as socialism, since the government or people do not collectively own the primary systems of wealth generation of products and services. Instead, the cost of social programs is paid for through the taxation generated by tens of thousands of privately owned small businesses and large corporations.

Current globalism fails economics 101 because they do not understand (or don't care) that individual liberty, the separation of powers, and capitalism, are inextricably bound in the creation and maintenance of wealth for the masses. Beyond bartering (which generates no real progressive wealth), there are only two general economic philosophies... with socialism (a command economy) being collective/government ownership...and capitalism (a market economy) being private ownership. All economic engines that run a large country or territory have an emphasis on one or the other. These are sometimes ambiguously termed "mixed economies". I disagree with this characterization. Democracies, republics, monarchies, oligarchies, etc. are superimposed political systems... that are run primarily by one or the other.

Regarding those who would change America's government and economic system...they should realize that *privatization* is how capitalism generates vast wealth to create a path for lower-classes to obtain a middle or upper-class status. As stated previously...social programs that assist the less fortunate in America are paid for through the taxation of these great wealth builders. America's system is best to build wealth as long as the "virtue" of the people is maintained through a morality that values fidelity, charitable causes, and a strong work ethic. The U.S. is the single great system for providing for the wealth and privileges of mass populations...and has been used as a model by many successful countries since its creation. Unfortunately, many of the rich who use tax shelters...are those unwilling to contribute back to society through a fair taxation.

Marxism

In Marxist theory, Socialism is the stage that follows Capitalism in the transition of a society to Communism, characterized by the implementation of collectivist principles. It is a theory or system of social organization in which the means of production and distribution of goods are owned and controlled either collectively or by the government. Karl Marx developed this (backward) theory based on the idea that "class struggle" was what was behind social-economic inequalities (unequal is not always a bad thing) among the masses. Marx believed that social and economic superstructures that "presumably" control the lower class (who built the substructure), are the natural result of a society that builds a (bourgeois) middle class. However, "struggle" is actually what creates opportunity for personal growth, advancement, and success. As well, supposed control by a middle-class is neither the motive nor the cause of inequality. Most middle-class people don't care...as they are basically content. In addition, Marx's theory on the so-called exploitation of labor and labor value makes no sense in light of modern economics.

One should understand the environment that Marx grew up in was under a corrupt Tsar and exploitative working conditions. However, his cynical idea of the middle-class creating "fabricated wants" for consumers to keep them distracted from being oppressed, misses the mark in a logical analysis. All wants in life are "fabricated", and if people are getting their wants met, that is not the definition of oppression. Marx felt ideologies are a bad thing...yet Marxism is ideological. Regardless, the moral thinking behind Marxism is pretentious and flawed...as it sacrifices individual freedoms and initiative in order to be "fair" to everyone. In reality, the application of this theory of "forced" equality has nothing to do with fairness (*as different individuals have different needs and wants for different materials and different conditions*). This flawed thinking destroys any hope for wealth or liberty for the masses. Socialism has always had a basic economic calculation problem that it ignores..."the market price system is an expression of *praxeology* [conceptual analysis and logical implications of preference, choice, means-end schemes, and so forth] and can not be replicated by any form of bureaucracy". (*Wikipedia-Mises, 21, 1951*)

Certain world leaders applied various political philosophies and strategies of their own devising to Marxist theory, using force and religious suppression with brutal results. The *Communist Manifesto* expresses the aim of the implied "superior" communist leaders to protect the working class, and to overthrow world-wide any political mechanisms that attempt to build a middle class. (*Marx, 22, 1848*) Beyond its implication of the low value of family and low expectations of the individual, there is endless historical evidence that a forced monetary equality in treatment of individuals does not lead them to respond in a fair or productive manner. This approach does nothing to inspire within people a strong sense of industry, ambition, and anticipation, for the reward would be the same no matter how hard, lazily, smartly, or foolishly one worked.

Marxism also makes a false correlation between master and servant. (domination is wrongly associated to master). That servitude is something "dominated" over...like slavery, for example...is incorrect. If domination exist, then that is slavery, not service. Service is a great attribute where fair compensation is granted, with the servant often becoming the master. That is inherent in its meaning. The irony is...Marxism supports domination. Read this statement on Marxist-Lenin philosophy in support of Communism: "...*cultural hegemony* is the domination of a culturally diverse society by the ruling class, who manipulate the culture of that society—the beliefs, explanations, perceptions, values, and mores—so that their imposed, ruling-class worldview becomes the accepted cultural norm; the universally valid dominant ideology, which justifies the social, political, and economic status quo as natural and inevitable, perpetual and beneficial for everyone, *rather* than as artificial social constructs that benefit only the ruling class." (*Wikipedia, 23, undated*) The clever deception here is that what is described in the former part of the paragraph is exactly what is described in the last phrase of the same paragraph. Socialist hegemony <u>is</u> an "*artificial social construct that benefits only the ruling class*".

Marxism cannot realistically take into account the realities of human psychology...including the flex for self-preservation, the need for striving, natural self-interests, aspirations, incentive and other healthy motivations...instead assuming these are human flaws in the face of a supposed greater nihilistic purpose (involving a baseless and blind sacrifice) exclusively for a nation-state or god-leader. Like Fascism, Communism is also oblivious to either personal merit or spiritual development. Those who understand human nature and history know that communism ultimately leads to Orwellian social conditions.

Some deeply misguided leaders and social philosophers wish to believe that if religion (and science in many cases) were abolished and replaced with a more singular concern for an earthly agenda of peace and sharing, everyone would be reasonable and cooperate. It is meant to be a simplistic solution to organizational complexities in large disparate populations. In the final analysis, Marxism is a remarkably narrow and shortsighted view that ignores general life ambiguities, individualism, variances in human maturation, freedom, and free will. Marxism essentially fails to acknowledge and address the complexity of the human condition. On the other hand, *Classic* Capitalism acknowledges and addresses this complexity while enabling a humane and worthwhile quality of life for the masses. And...as much as socialists find it distastefully ambiguous, successful economics is reliant...even based on...faith. This *faith constant* can't be substituted by anything in an economic equation.

U.S. Constitution under Attack

Today there are two notable attempts to achieve a political globalism...a secular Socialist agenda and a theocratic Islamic agenda. There is no apparent democratic (majority rule) or republican (minority representation) process in either of these globalisms...and...implementation of an agenda is often carried out behind closed doors by a self-appointed select few sovereigns...putting themselves in charge to decide the issues and vote them into international law without any (rule-of-law) applied to themselves. In parallel with this, there is a general three-pronged attack to destroy the U.S. Constitution's essential principles. The first attack is from ignorance, anger, and immorality of Modern Liberalism...

which also leans to the Left's secular socialist agenda. The second attack is the extreme hatred and fear behind religious terrorism...with its own agenda for a forced theocratic globalism. The third general attack is the greed and control of elitists fueling a globalism (that would be under their control)...often with the pretense of helping the secular socialists. How do they operate? It is simple...half-truths are designed to confuse the issues. Confusion leads to fear. Fear leads to anger. Anger leads to war. War leads to distraction.

This last group is suggested by some to be composed of an American political deep state, and a global shadow government of elites...which are in league. It is also suggested by many...that it is this American elite class is who really pulls the political strings in America...regardless of who is elected to the U. S. Presidential office. However, a President who is independent of their influence would be perceived as a dire threat. Their objective is to maintain power and control, whether it is right or wrong, and will use whatever means possible and necessary. Studies have identified some 50 plus families in the United States that control the larger political environment. Several thousand more influence various states. I do not name the names or the studies here...they can easily be googled. Nevertheless, Americans are resilient.

A civilization that chooses high morals, ethical standards, good values, and liberty is one of staying power and thrives. One of low or absent morals, standards and liberty has no staying power...and ultimately suffers before eventually dying. This condition is reflected in civilizations today and of the past...and in certain religious and secular regions with practices that do not value the challenging co-existence of liberty and morality. The result is many spots of degradation in the hodge podge of today's global society. Radical groups...from disenfranchised and disaffected subcultures, regions, or countries...seek desperately to overtake the resources of free advanced countries by subterfuge or violent force, resulting in an endless cycle of suffering.

People can change. Integrity in one's personal spiritual or religious practice is essential. True religion, in part of whatever it may ultimately be, will recognize the inherent agency of mankind. that...while we will have the consequences of our actions sooner or later, individuals will be free to make choices that lead to those consequences, good or bad. God can provide a program for our progress, yet he will never force us to choose it. For one to be forced into submission to either good or evil has no purpose or meaning for the individual. The various machinations of American society that allow for greater freedoms, leads to the greater capacity for both good and evil to operate...as they are expected to. That is, individuals must be tested...to show they are willing within and of themselves...to do good, and to learn to do better by the dictates of their own conscience. Only a land of liberty and opportunity fully provides this environment of choice and consequence. With it comes great a responsibility for choosing wisely and righteously.

Socialism and Centralization

In contrast to capitalism, which ebbs with the tides of time and change, the effect of socialism is to naturally trend toward centralizing political and economic control under a rigid and static authority. This leads to combining and centralizing the economy and government into one insular and protected group of powerful controllers...without natural or organized "watchdog" entities...or a separation of powers to mitigate unethical actions. This is why socialism is compatible with communism. Both are structurally static and simplistic. The politics are simplified. Communism believes in only two political classes, the workers and the (supposedly benevolent) controllers. However, such social collectives of resources and centralization of power is highly constrictive to human development and progress and, therefore, dangerously adverse to human nature.

Socialism leads to a stifling, overarching centralization, and therefore, limitation of material goods and services development. As such, it cannot accommodate much free thought, expression, and actions for the masses. For example, It restricts and discourages intellectual property ownership, and therefore...discovery and invention are restrained and impeded. Prohibition of land ownership prevents ongoing discovery and innovation. Flexibilities are suffocated in trade, commerce, creative transactions, and the vast opportunities for various distribution channels. Unlike free market capitalism, which leaves the economy to chance and opportunity, socialism does not teach natural cooperation, or accommodate the many unique variances in economic or personal life pursuits, to meet variable needs or wants.

Growth and character development through personal accomplishment and reward is not something much valued in such controlled states. Obedience to the controllers is highly valued (by the state). Althusius concept of *consociation* is completely ignored (the importance of levels of social units...starting with the nuclear family). In contrast, the Communist Manifesto considers the nuclear family a detriment to society. Eventually, however, basic human needs for freedom, family, and pursuit start to kick in. In turn, the government eventually panics and becomes oppressive...because it's limited makeup fails (is unable) to acknowledge and accommodate the complexities and capacities of the individuals amongst the masses. Absent any separation of powers, their supposed authority can no longer protect them from suspicion, anarchy, and eventual revolution.

This is why socialism it is incredibly dangerous not only to those who implement it, but to the individual liberties and general happiness of the populace. Anyone who wavers from the path of the self-appointed controllers (which are nearly always guaranteed to be corrupt...as absolute power corrupts absolutely), the price shall be costly to all. The narrow, ignorant, arrogant, flawed, baseless, and misguided assumption that all people should be equal in all things, even though the reality is there are vast disparities in individuals in terms of their needs, wants, preferences, beliefs, motives, merits, etc. has led historically to incomprehensible suffering. Socialism has proven time and again to be far too narrow to accommodate the freedoms people need to pursue their various and diverse economic paths to personal happiness.

Socialism, Faith, and Merit

Following is an example to explain how some capitalists see another major flaw in socialism, and why it's attempts at an economy-base collective and centralization endlessly fails. *A conversation between two socialists named Me and You*:

> **Me**: I will create a perfect society, or close to it...because I am smart enough.

> <u>You</u>: Yes, a peaceful and harmonious society is a good idea. I will help you.

> **Me**: How can you help me? I am smarter than you.

> <u>You</u>: Not true, I am as smart or smarter than you.

> **Me**: No...I know what to do, and everyone must be agreeable with me, or it won't work.

> <u>You</u>: Well, I know what needs to be done, as well.

> **Me**: I must be the shepherd and you must be the sheep.

<u>You</u>: Why must I be the sheep and you the shepard?

Me: Because I am smarter than you. You are not co-operating...and must be subdued.

<u>You</u>: I will fight you to the death so that "true" socialism will prevail.

Me: You shall die in jail as my political prisoner.

<u>You</u>: (Thinks of where to find a gun shop)

Intervening Capitalist: Whoa there...what goes?

Me and <u>You</u>: (Looking at each other) It is the evil capitalist, says **Me**. <u>You</u> nods in agreement.

Me: We must destroy your evil merit system before we destroy each other.

Capitalist: What is wrong with merit? Do we not act to succeed?

<u>You</u>: It is wrong of you to act to succeed. What about those that don't? It's not fair.

Capitalist: Should we not leave the results of our acts to God? Then help others?

Me and <u>You</u>: (In unison) There is no god.

Capitalist: If there be no God, then who is to decide

what absolutes there are to base a law on?

Me and <u>You</u>: (Look at each other, than in unison) I will decide what is right.

<u>You</u> than **Me**: (Look at each other, angrily) No...I will decide...no...I will decide.

Me and <u>You</u>: (Both thinking where the nearest gun shop is)

Capitalist: (Observing) hm...I think maybe socialism is a bad idea.

Whether you are agreeable with this little scenario or not, historically...godless socialism (I do not mean to imply people who are socialists are godless...just the concept) has only spawned war, even amongst themselves. Other than envious misguided complaints about different "classes" of wealth, there is very little to give socialism any kind of lasting foundation...because there is no absolute in belief in anything beyond the temporary. Anything and everything is subject to change by the whims of whoever is in charge...which makes a stable and functional centralization perpetually impossible. This is its biggest flaw among many flaws. By its own nature socialism can't be fixed...nor the suffering that comes with it.

There are those who may point to so-called *religious socialism*. Such a thing could only exist in a pure theocracy...which America is not. The whole point being, as I stated at the beginning, the idea is not the problem, people are the problem. Most people are not "celestial beings of purity"...and unless you and everyone around you is..it is never going to work. There is no secret formula of social and genetic engineering that circumvents our collective spiritual shortcomings. However, we can collectively "choose" to pursue a virtuous life and society.

Socialism and Education

Centralizing educational initiatives at the federal level has been disastrous for American education. The founders, no doubt, left education out of the U.S. Constitution assuming no one in their right mind would be foolish enough to try legislating and regulating it (similar to attempting to legislate morality when people have different values). Federal involvement in education is almost always misguided and results in dumbing down the populace, wasting billions of dollars. Education...for it to be practical and productive, is necessarily married to local economies and resources. No one wants to pay for an education system that produces dysfunctional people.

The multi-functional elements and currents of a large, disparate market economy are intellectually overwhelming...especially for geographically distanced government office workers. Federal officers generally know next to nothing about the various on-site operations, timely decision-making variables in resource allocations, commercial patterns, distribution channels, state codes, negotiations, contracting, etc.,...of a multitude of interlocking industries, business functions, and other localized microeconomic considerations. To understand the macroeconomic environment is to understand the curricular demands needed for market-ready students.

A practical education can be found in the sovereignty of the individual states. Common Core and its weak attempt to isolate universal core intelligence factors to meet the demands of higher education and economy...like many failed socialist tendencies toward centralization, collectives, and uniformity,...will never account for variances due to the complexities, speed of changing market forces, and human capital that are beyond any economic forecasting and predictive capacities.

Naturally, mass population psychologies and their engagements influence a multitude of ever-changing and interconnected macro and micro economic currents every day.

In America, primary education should only and ever be the responsibility of the individual states and a student's respective guardianship. Family is essential. As stated by Auguste Comte, a French philosopher of the 19th century,…"The tendency to attack the family is a symptom of social chaos". (*see reference 8*) As well, states and reservations have different economies, population characteristics, traditions, subcultures, demographics, industries, commerce, geologic resources, geographic boundaries, climates, and so on. Every school board should choose and maintain curricula germane to the local, state, (and its uniquely connected) international milieu. Those local learnings will be utilized more effectively on the international stage and markets...wherein the similarities and the differences in specific local and foreign economies are targeted and mitigated for the best transmission of information and commodities for foreign and interstate commerce.

The misguided emphasis in uniformity in common core theory is additionally detrimental to children absorbing information with variable and unique cognitive styles. Common Core has also subversively put it's socialistic public school teachings over God, in its science and social curricula...where neither should show up. This insulting misapplication by our government...using so-called uniform testing criteria, to apply what is not...and never will be…"uniform", has caused far more damage to the individual academic, spiritual, and economic proficiencies of many more students than it ever helped. Education, like capitalism, thrives on chance and opportunity combined with one's faith in the virtues and unique complexities of the individual within the ecosystem.

Chapter 4

The Danger of Modern Liberalism

Take Care of Us

"Modern American Liberalism is the dominant version of liberalism in the United States. It is characterized by social liberalism, and combines ideas of civil liberty and equality with support for social justice and a mixed economy". (*Wikipedia, 24, undated*) Social liberals, therefore, look for a balance between individual liberty and social-economic equality. However, liberty...by its very definition...is in contradiction to this equality. Modern Liberalism incorrectly assumes constitutional equality goes beyond opportunity...circumventing freedoms, merit, risks, consequences, etc., thereby forcing results that don't reflect efforts or values. This disturbing and self-contradicting idea trends to socialism and the Left. This would in effect...be the opposite of so-called "social justice". Today's liberalism has little to do with *classical liberalism*, which championed individualism and a free economy.

What is equality? Equality under the law is good. Equality in opportunity is also a good goal. Depending on context and application, equality in general is not a good thing. For example, not everyone's medical needs are the same. Equality in medical expenditures would be inhumane to those who have greater medical needs. Britain's socialized healthcare system is an example of a system controlling individuals rather than individuals controlling the system. In the case of *Alfie Evens*, this collective government mentality prevented the parents from independently seeking help from the U.S., which had medical experts offering to help the parents...and give their child a chance at life. To save face with their socialized medicine, Britain prevented the U.S. from providing any medical intervention. Rationing as a form of equality will always lead to loss of hope with dire results for a society.

Ludwig Von Mises states regarding the confused social democrats..."If anyone likes to call a social Ideal which retains private ownership in the means of production socialistic, why, let him!" "A man may call a cat a dog and the sun the moon if it pleases him. However, it does no good and only creates misunderstanding." He states that adding religion doesn't change socialism, and noble motives doesn't change it...it is still socialism. "The planned economy which the advocates of dictatorship wish to set up is as precisely as socialistic as the socialism propagated by the self-styled social democrats." "When there is nationalization of the means of production, that is socialism. Whether it's lead by noble or ignoble people, it doesn't change its definition or its propensity to fail." (*Mises, 25, 1951*)

We are a self-governing people. Adams stated: "Our Constitution was made only for a moral and religious people. It is wholly inadequate to the government of any other." (*John Adams, 26, 1798*) In this light, I believe any supposed "relative" morality will ultimately doom us to the ash heap of history. Immorality begins the process of losing responsibility, and therefore, our freedoms. "The rise to power of the modern liberal agenda has resulted from the fact that the people of western societies have irrationally demanded that governments take care of them and manage their lives." (*Rossiter, Lyle Jr., M.D., 27, 2005*)

In such a circumstance, governing the people would be dependent on the "mood" of whoever is currently in charge. This singularity in sovereignty can only lead to hegemony and tyranny.

Is the goal of neo-liberalism, in establishing a global socialism...bent upon achieving the lowest possible common denominator in Christian morality...and then making it disappear altogether? It appears so. Purposefully confusing vocabulary, oversimplification, self-victimization, fake news, and false entitlement, are examples of the propaganda tools in their toolbox of tactical disinformation to affect modern liberal sentiment for socialism. A lot of the political resentment now coming from the Left and modern liberals can only be interpreted as "let someone control us so we can self-destruct...then take the rest of you down with us".

Modern liberals also complain about our legal system being unfair. This is sometimes justified. However, our current legal justice system is the closest humans are going to get to social justice. It is because humans are imperfect and often corrupt. There may be policies and procedures that need changing, still, our current system is fundamentally sound. However, something *is and has been* wrong...with many of those running that system...who poorly implement or circumvent the law. Apparently, those lawkeepers responsible for holding the lawbreakers accountable are not doing so...often breaking the law themselves. This is a people problem...mainly a lack of integrity and virtue...making them incapable of rendering true justice and mercy. The system is not at fault, and there is not a better one in existence...but those running it are becoming increasingly less worthy of it. Other nations may be better at punishing the guilty, but not at excusing the innocent. Regardless, If our virtue fails us...so will a superior system.

Weaver wrote in THE MAINSPRING OF HUMAN PROGRESS: "Most of the major ills of the world have been caused by well-meaning people who ignored the principle of individual freedom, except as applied to themselves, and who were obsessed with fanatical zeal to improve the lot of mankind-in-the-mass through some pet formula of their own…the harm done by ordinary criminals, murderers, gangsters, and thieves is negligible in comparison with the agony inflicted upon human beings by the professional do-gooders, who attempt to set themselves up as gods on earth and who would ruthlessly force their views on all others – with the abiding assurance that the end justifies the means." (*Henry Grady Weaver, 28, 1999*) Within these last few paragraphs lies the dynamic that leads to socialism. Weariness in moral responsibility while craving a false sense of entitlement and security in one (large) group of people, coupled with a narcissistic lust for power and control in another (small) group of people.

Intellectualism

Regarding modern Intellectualism…Thomas Sowell argued that there can be good cause for distrust of intellectuals. When working in their fields of expertise, many intellectuals have increased knowledge. However, when compared to other careers, Sowell suggests intellectuals have few disincentives for speaking outside their expertise, and are less likely to face the consequences of their errors. For example, "a physician is judged by effective treatment, yet might face malpractice lawsuits if he or she harms a patient. In contrast, a university professor with tenure is far less likely to be judged by the effectiveness of his ideas and far less likely to face repercussions for his or her errors". (*Thomas Sowell, 29, 2010*)

Sowell continues…"By encouraging, or even requiring, students to take stands where they have neither the knowledge nor the intellectual training to seriously examine complex issues, teachers promote the expression of unsubstantiated opinions, the venting of uninformed emotions, and the habit of acting on those opinions and emotions, while ignoring or dismissing opposing views, without having either the intellectual equipment or the personal experience to weigh one view against another in any serious way."

Sowell discusses intellectual influence, labeling school teachers as what he calls "intelligentsia" who recruit children, beginning in elementary school, to advocate for or against issues as part of "community service" projects, which will later assist them in the college application process. In this manner, intellectuals participate in other areas where they may possess no prior knowledge at all in order to influence public policy issues. The author argues that as a result, they encourage their students to formulate opinions "without any intellectual training or prior knowledge of those issues, making constraints against falsity few or non-existent".

Similar arguments have been made by others. Historian Paul Johnson argued that a close examination of 20th-century history reveals that intellectuals have championed innumerable disastrous public policies, writing..."Beware intellectuals". Not merely should they be kept well away from the levers of power, they should also be objects of suspicion when they seek to offer collective advice." (*Paul Johnson, 30, 2007*) Journalist Wolfe described an intellectual as "a person knowledgeable in one field who speaks out only in others". (*Tom Wolfe, 31, 2000*) The history of the world documents the struggles of human beings to escape from tyrannies of all types (as influenced and supported by "intellectuals"), whether imposed by brute force and declared entitlement of a dictator, or justified by economic, religious or political sophistries.

Some sociologists posit that "the elevation of reason over other human values tends to treat people as a means to an end, and elevates *progress* to an unquestioned good." (*Adorno, T. Horkheimer, M., 32, 1972*) *Frankfurt School, rationalwiki.org*) Reason has its place, but never should it come before human traits such as compassion, forgiveness, and love. Because all humans are of great worth, these traits should never be ignored just because someone wants his or her reasoning to reach a certain outcome. Without a spiritual and virtuous context of consideration, understanding and wisdom will fail. One will end up contributing...even consenting...to horrific circumstances.

Alinsky and Community Organizing

Saul Alinsky's philosophy teaches community organizing as a neo-Marxist strategy for those unwilling to meet the demands and responsibilities of the American market system...to create enough public discord to distract the general public from its concurrent infiltrations into the various social, media, military, sports, commercial, entertainment, and political systems. Alinsky even noted in writing he owes part of his approach to Lucifer (Satan), real or not. (*Alinsky, 33, 1971*) His ideology of using evil to fight evil has left a path of social destruction due to its nature of rationalizing wrong in accomplishing change. Paul warned the Roman saints of the same tactic.

Paul writes about the justification of the law and those who are unrighteous in abusing it. He specifies those who say to themselves "Let us do evil, that good may come? whose damnation is just." (*Romans 3:8*) Paul is saying that it is wrong to use evil to accomplish good...that is never how good is accomplished. It also results in the damnation (stopping of progress) of the people doing such evil...unless they repent. In my opinion, the idea of a socialistic globalism was planned in the seditious Democratic National Convention echelons of power...in concert with the UN...long before. They have used Alinsky's philosophy of "divide and conquer" to insidiously achieve their goals. Examples of strategy are...if you repeat a lie often enough people will begin to believe it...and, advancing an agenda by expanding the meaning of a word to vilify and dehumanize...i.e. conservatives are Nazis.

Most of us want the world to work in peace and harmony. However, when one wants a flawed ideal like socialism to succeed, one needs to truly examine one's motives. Is it to achieve an "outward" appearance of peace and then take personal glory in a temporary, yet misguided adoration by peers and admirers? A stable external peace must emanate from the internal peace of individuals. One cannot experience internal peace without good personal decisions. Its absence is a warning that something is wrong. Demanding the immediate result of an external utopia...devoid of compassion, logic, and coherence is self-defeating. One cannot create solutions by cherry-picking favorite personal thoughts that fail to address reality. That is pretty much the definition of psychosis.

In addition to Modern Liberalism, Radical Islam has been working for the last few decades to friend the Left and Progressive movements because they see the Left as a source for weakening the U.S. and its Constitution. They have thus, along with many Alinsky followers, infiltrated into many levels of our government, business, media, sports, military and educational systems. The radical's reasoning is...if we can use the weak to buffer us from the strong, we can more easily attack the strong, and later destroy the weak. A former U.S. president (perhaps well meaning, but truly misguided) sought to undermine U.S. Constitutional law and intimidate U.S. legal authority, while attempting to subtly transition American society to function under U.N. international law. *(Time: United Nations speech transcript, 34, 2016)*

Many personalities of the Alinsky persuasion have a dysfunctional (path-of-least-effort) desire for a singular order to maintain control for them over the volatile external world. Since such personalities often cannot control or discipline themselves, they seek a "caretaker". The caretakers would be those narcissists who are happy to oblige. The compelling desire to centralize everything around oneself or one's way of thinking is predominant in the psychopathology of narcissistic personality disorder (NPD). It is complementary...even symbiotic...with the aforementioned passive personalities. (*Antisocial Personality Disorders, 35, 2000*) This becomes a dysfunctional codependent relationship. It represents the path of least resistance and of personal effort for both personality types, and is characteristic of societies trending toward the pure centralization of Socialism.

A complimentary anomaly to Alinsky's philosophy is called *Effective Altruism*. It is a form of self-justification popular within the elite modern liberal establishment. Flawed and contradictory in its logic...it teaches that to circumvent corrupt government, one should focus on becoming rich and then contribute to select charities without the interference of politics. Usually, it does just the opposite...as by circumventing government...one makes it less effective and accountable to the rule of law, and to the people. Unfortunately, this *catch-22* just leads to more dark politics, since the effect of giving vast amounts of money and resources to another entity portends entitlements be given to the contributor in return. In addition...going this route leads to the initial intent of the altruistic individual falling to the lure of power and influence that comes with vast personal wealth. (*Burns, 36, 2018*)

Being charitable in this manner will never be a substitute for the virtue of individuals. Effective Altruism is just another excuse for greed and self-deception. Certain political groups push the socialist agenda in colleges under the auspices of this philosophy. Often, it is those with limited classes on economics or constitutional law. They may never understand the reality that one cannot "manufacture" or "engineer" freedom and prosperity...that its society-wide existence...is always *incidental* to the virtue, freedom, faith, work ethic and good values of the people. Just being charitable in isolation of personal virtues is not sustainable for successful future generations.

ANTIFA, Nazism, and Socialism

Karl Marx, a sociologist in the mid 19th Century, and Friedrich Engels...developed the theory of Communism in response to the poverty and oppression under a Tsarist ruled Empire. It was about establishing collective property and a classless society, with the education of the communists to control the workers. They believed capitalism created classes which impoverished the general workers in the mines, factories, and farms of the day. Socialism came about in this early and rigorous industrial age. However, the failure of communist governments to live up to the ideal of a communist society as well as their natural trend towards increasing authoritarianism, has been linked to the decline of communism in the late 20th century.

In 1917, the Bolshevik Party seized power during the Russian Revolution and created the Soviet Union, the world's first Marxist state. The doctrine implied expansionism and world domination. Therefore, many spies were sent covertly to America during the Cold War. Demographers have estimated (a conservative estimate - *Genocide Convention*) that self-styled communist governments have collectively claimed the lives of more than 68 million people through starvation, political purges, extrajudicial killings, forced labour camps, and violently implemented social engineering policies. (*Wikipedia, 37, undated*)

Adolf Hitler and Nazism has a more complex history involving the exceptionalisms of Fichte, Kant, and Nauman, the last of whom tried to combine nationalism and socialism, with its socialism being distinct from Marxist socialism, mostly in that it was race-based. This combination of exceptionalism, nationalism, and socialism resulted in the volatile philosophy of Nazism which made no room for anyone other than a supreme race. There is a vast difference in the concept of American exceptionalism. American exceptionalism is not based on race, but rather on moral character and merit...in other words, Christian principles of work, charity, love, service to others, etc., a wholly different paradigm. Nazism, by contrast, is anti-Semitic, anti-Catholic...anti-everything that was not part of that supposedly supreme race.

How can war and mass-murder possibly be avoided with NAZI doctrine? How can war be avoided with Marxism, which implies expansionism and world domination as standard operating procedure? Hitler hated the Bolsheviks, and they hated Hitler in return...but they had a fair understanding of each other...much as do the Communists ANTIFA (Anti-Fascist), and the NAZI (Supremacists) in America. "The **Battle of Stalingrad** (23 August 1942 – 2 February 1943) was the largest confrontation of World War II, in which Germany and its allies fought the Soviet Union for control of the city of Stalingrad (now Volgograd) in Southern Russia. Marked by 5 months of fierce close quarters combat and direct assaults on civilians in air raids, it was the largest (nearly 2.2 million personnel) and bloodiest (1.8–2 million killed, wounded or captured) battle in the history of warfare. After their defeat at Stalingrad, the German High Command had to withdraw vast military forces from the Western Front to replace their losses." (*Wikipedia free encyclopedia, 38, undated*)

These same two groups in America create chaos and violence with funding at the behest of godless men of great wealth. In coalescence, mainstream media organizations today more often support the Left. They manipulate the meaning of a word to be exclusively contrived to their political paradigm. The acronym ANTIFA becomes inclusive of all progressives, the word NAZI becomes inclusive of all conservatives, because they know many people like to dichotomize for easier intellectual consumption. Both sides could receive funding from the elite to draw people into chaos, while keeping the elite's hold on power in the shadows. Their hope is that the average person in America will be drawn into one or the other of these black holes of socialism, diverting the population's attention from themselves. In any case, virtue will never be found in either Communism or Nazism. The reality is socialism always leads to extremism.

Chapter 5

Communication Breakdown

A Global Shockwave

With the invention of the internet, the computer ushered in the information age. This was an age like no other experienced by the world. The resulting globalism created multiple culture and future shocks as different cultures were connected like at no other time in history. *Culture Shock* is defined as "the feeling of disorientation experienced by someone who is suddenly subjected to an unfamiliar culture, way of life, or set of attitudes". *Future Shock* is defined by the Tofflers in their book of the same name as "too much change in too short a period of time". As well, information technologies grew in sophistication, and sedentary forms of entertainment grew exponentially. The way tens millions of people interacted and socialized was changed forever.

While the potential for a lot of bad came from this, the potential for much good also came. Like most technology, what you do with it determines whether it is good or bad. The bad might be...easy access to pornography, greater means to infidelity in relationships, exposure to uninformed extremist views, and a myriad of scammers, trollers, predators, dark web activities, etc. The good might be infinite business opportunities, greater family connections, better communication with all kinds of people and professions, easier research, etc.. Indeed, the power of the computerized internet is astonishing in its ability to accomplish both good and evil.

Propaganda vs. Journalism

There has always been propaganda and journalism. The first attempts to persuade and the second attempts to report. Since the sensationalizing advent [1895–1898] of "yellow journalism" neither can be reliably bifurcated from modern mainstream media. (*The term originated in the competition over the New York City newspaper market between major newspaper publishers Joseph Pulitzer and William Randolph Hearst...google search*) Today, deadlines imposed by intangible market forces lead to speed-induced sound bites and minute commentaries. Those who control the media programming may believe most of the population is too busy with their personal lives...to develop an appetite for a politically astute and accurate view of the world. They figure most people would prefer escapism to realism. This could be true. Nonetheless, programmers and producers helped create *infotainment* as a way to emphasize the use of information (whether propaganda or journalism) as a primary means to monetize and entertain, rather than inform. The motivation here is strictly economic survival and profit. The specific content provided, however, runs the gamut of good to evil.

Propaganda machines with an agenda are in the mainstream media today posing as objective journalistic news organizations. Having long ago abandoned integrity and accountability, they will reinforce a viewpoint by manipulating appearances in a manner that attempts to convince consumers and viewers that the amount of support a particular position, person or practice has...is much greater or less than it really is. To hopefully affect a sort of mass *self-fulfilling prophecy* from viewers...there are a number of techniques and technologies to apply in modern audio-visual tactics. One might pan over smaller groups in a way that a camera limits or avoids empty space. One could deceptively time the filming before or after an event. A reporter may use semantics filled with superlatives to distort perceptions that will influence a perspective.

False journalists will take every subtle tool of influence used in propaganda to suggest representation where it does not exist. These are pre-emptive attempts to employ psychology in hopes the public will somehow manufacture and adopt this media's preferred world view. However, the principal responsibility of a journalist is to report...not influence. Journalists who hide their personal agenda and bias while feigning fairness and accuracy are guilty of deception. Every day, the mass media continues to bombard us with misleading, inadequate, arbitrary, and contradictory information. It is a monumental effort in not allowing oneself to become confused, disoriented, and manipulated by either unintentional misinformation or intentional disinformation.

Other ethical concerns include media using other media as a source...as opposed to an actual origin...often using weak or biased sampling methodology and models, accompanied by meaningless predictions and conclusions. There is an obvious bias in the conscious use of loaded questions, employing "hot button" word lists, and selectively interviewing only those who will substantiate the news station's preferred narrative. This reflects a major trend towards propaganda...not reporting. The social impact, as the public absorbs this bad information...is catastrophic. Virtue is lost in abundance.

Ethics, Media and Youth

Much of today's mass cable or satellite media transmission (as received by Radio, TV or Internet) is geared to fabricating artificial soap operas or superficial emotional drama. They accompany this with brazen dialogue, obscene visuals, innuendo, and editing tactics (or lack thereof) for maximum shock value. Some may consider this is content not to be taken seriously; however, the cumulative effect of constant exposure to this material will have, in the very least, a *net* negative impact on one's general perspective, attitude, and disposition.

Youth without experience, supervision, or protection through censure, may trend suicidal. Over a moderate period of time, the impact is the mass desensitization of entire generations of people who become indifferent, jaded, and uninspired as adults. Business opportunists, at times funded by the various underworlds and black markets (illicit drugs, sex-slavery, gun running, blood diamonds, commercial pirating, etc.) in order to generate fast and vast wealth, don't want the general parental population to be aware of their multi-media involvement and influence through electronic games, music, etc., and its impact on susceptible youth.

The Entertainment Industry
I believe few would disagree that the media and entertainment industries are copious with narcissists, histrionics, predators...and the like. By targeting and appealing to the natural curiosity and taking advantage of the socio-biological immaturities of young people...warped producers of films, reality shows, and electronic games that include gratuitous amounts of nudity, sex, intense gore, ultra-violence, abrasive language, drug use, and indifferent or abnormal social behaviors...are able to easily attract those youth who are neglected and rebellious, as well as impact those youth who are highly impressionable.

Judging by the material in some of the more current horror films, some producers in the entertainment business are apparently indifferent towards humanity...full of rage, misery and revenge. My guess is they must laugh at their destruction of the sensibilities in youth, portraying people as nothing more than mindless sheep, who deserve to be taken advantage of and slaughtered. After all, it's a well-received idea that misery loves company.

Entertainment magazines (cyberspace and hardcopy) are embedded in media programming and marketing...presenting the Stars of disturbing movies, games, and reality "docudramas", as role models and heroes... their influence reaching into households unable to control the mass of electronic media coming from every direction. Latch-key kids, street children, and youth without a healthy schedule of activities or mature adult supervision...are left to their own devices, and exposed haphazardly and incidentally to the harsh stimuli they absorb. The young have no way of comprehending or processing such stimuli in a safe and appropriate manner.

Great danger lies in Internet social media such as Facebook, YouTube and Twitter. Information is not filtered through any truly secure protocol to intercept and determine its degree of safety and reliability. With the free flow of data streams, privacy and reputation is easily destroyed through betrayal, mistakes, or poor judgment. Receptive information is often one-sided and polarized. Cyber bullying, trolling, and predatory practices go unmitigated without the typical socio-physical buffers that allow the actual presence of others who care, to provide equalizing responses and physical intercession.

Free Will and Choice
It is true these inexperienced youth possess free will, however, before free will can be operated on in an intelligent manner, there must be an environment created in which a child can observe, experience, and act upon the wholesome and fun activities and groups that a neighborhood and community has to offer. Any competent professional psychologist will tell you children need protective boundaries because they have not yet matured enough to handle all the material presented in the adult

world. Studies suggest that while teens demonstrate certain cognitive maturities, their emotional maturity lags far behind. (*Steinburg, et al, 39, 2009*)

This means many youth are being exposed to material and stimuli they cannot emotionally understand and process, to properly operate their free will upon it. But operate it, they will. A truly civilized society would consider that any environment of perpetual negative thinking or on-going dark stimulus from the mass media would eventually impact a child, even in the presence of other wholesome material. The existence of the dark side of society should be obvious to those who witness the growing populations in our youth detentions, young men and women in our penitentiaries, and those now operating in various criminal networks. Social engineering, no matter how intricate and well-meaning, will not solve this issue alone. The only true answer for these individuals is to help them find virtue within themselves.

Chapter 6

Academics in Regression

Secular Teaching

Secular academia often treats history as a static linear process of human development and, as a so-called progression from the religious to the secular. However, this is not what modern science supports. Archeology and Anthropology point to ancient civilizations that were politically, spiritually, and technologically more advanced than their contemporaries. This includes many of our current or recent civilizations. Advanced and primitive civilizations are sporadic through time. The adoption of the word "realism" by today's secularists, to distinguish themselves from the supposed "myths" of religious thought and history is, at best, ambiguous. They also erroneously assume a monopoly on science. Yet with science, the unseen reality is infinitely more prevalent than the seen...the unknown than the known.

It is also true that much human knowledge in various fields of past learning endeavors has been lost in time. The great fire of Alexandria from the Battle of Dyrrhachium, for example, destroyed vast volumes of information, much of it yet unconsolidated...ancient world truths in the arts and sciences...that modern civilization may never recover.

Rather, history seems to be a cycle or fluctuations of dark ages and enlightened golden ages...geographically dispersed in different periods throughout the course of known time. Perhaps by learning virtue we can evolve a humble process of cutting through the fog of modern day half-truths and deceptions...becoming better and wiser through the personal rediscovery of ancient and eternal truths.

Attitude and Social Extremes

In 1984 I was student teaching in an educational resource room setting in Utah, and was asked to help a young girl with a mild intellectual impairment. She was having trouble understanding how five pennies could be worth the same as a nickel. The problem for her was *abstraction*. I needed to find a bridge from the concrete (five pennies and a nickel) to the abstract (1+1+1+1+1=5), so I asked her if she liked gum. She said yes, excitedly.

I then asked her if she had five sticks of gum and she put them all into a package of gum, how many packages would she have? Almost instantly a light went off in her head. With amazement she said "one!" She now understood, through a simple analogy, that although five pennies would not *concretely* fit inside a nickel, if pennies and a nickel were "like" the gum, the pennies could all fit inside (or equal) one nickel. With this approach she had bridged the concrete to the abstract.

Lev Vygotsky, a Russian psychologist, who analyzed the relationship between language and thought, concluded that most anyone could be taught the basics in most anything, if one could find the right motivation and approach. (*Vygotsky, 40, 1934*) The point here is, everyone can progress and have success in life. Every life has great worth and purpose. We can all use some help. This is an important attitude of humility to have towards others and oneself.

The same attitude applies to emotional learning. Because some individuals lack this virtue of humility...there is a dire consequence to their emotional intelligence. Unable to handle the ongoing life pressures...the conditions of fear, anger, annoyances, or impulsivities... are likely to trigger imbalance or rage at some point. Inadequacy in dealing with social and personal stressors may progress towards hatred...then violence. Those not dealing well with intense emotions in social settings may not have resolved personal issues or learned important coping skills. Humility helps us to be teachable and learnable. This is not a weakness.

This is not the only dynamic that leads to extremism. There also exists those individuals with *psychopathic* (not to be confused with *psychotic*) tendencies. Brain pathology research suggest there is a physiological difference in the amygdala of the temporal lobe...affecting conscience. Nevertheless, even for an individual like this, without learned moral inhibitions, selfishness will often lead to violent measures to obtain impulsive desires. In either case, whether violence is the outcome of rage or indifference, it is always at great cost to those on the receiving end...and ultimately destroys the perpetuator.

Individuals who refuse to acknowledge accountability for their rage or basic impulses...eventually look to external causations for blame. Many of them may form certain dysfunctional and disenfranchised associations which reinforce, reciprocate, and justify extremes in thought and behavior. These groups or organizations are inconsiderate and indifferent as to what "outsiders" might be thinking or feeling. This becomes an environment for spawning hatred and planned violence. These are generalizations...however, extremism in thought, expression, and action...which is rationalized...leads to racism, ethnic cleansing, anti-religious and anti-secular intolerances, discrimination, criminal organization, violent gangs, terrorism, fundamentalism, anarchy and a host of other social ills and evils.

Social extremism is a symptom of those seeking a shortcut and avoidance of life's difficult challenges. Extremism never leads to good character and happiness, and as such, it is evil. There are no easy outs to personal success and happiness; it takes learning and discipline toward good character development...regardless of one's experiences, resources, and past or present influences. *Moderation* and good attitude influences one's personal constitution, and develops a more positive and reflective disposition. Observing the values and principles in the U.S. Constitution is indeed a virtue that is the *moral backbone* of America.

Curricular Integrity and Extremism

Through past years of personal experience in various American academic institutions, I realized one of the things that hurts our education in a number of ways, are ideologically extreme educators and boards of education, who want to be "martyr's for a cause", to the detriment of those who must suffer their paternalistic, condescending, pedantic, biased, and limiting philosophies at the cost of a practical education. There are those individuals who should be in teaching, but they are disheartened and discouraged by a system full of dysfunctional, tenured armchair academicians. Beyond this, our basic education system is simply not pragmatic (and is dangerous) because so many curriculums are influenced by neoliberal ideological agendas along with lax moral standards in teachers. In addition, curricula are complicated with information overload.

A focus on the universal basics in applied-sciences, reading, writing, math, music, art, social studies, civics, computer literacy, and physical education are fundamental to normal and healthy human learning and development...but this focus on the individual has been lost. Many Educational Service Districts (ESDs) have antagonized the public with this loss of focus. Some have burned their political funding bridges to levy the general public for adequate educational funding. They have lost sight of...for many children...a well-rounded education that fosters general life appreciation, balance, and understanding. Public schools are for teaching children *how* to think, not *what* to think. It is understandable why watchdog groups are appalled with the lack of transmission of basic skills, fundamental knowledge, and useful intelligence, via the primary school system.

Although a good education does not guarantee a person will be "good", one possible catalyst into extremist thinking is indeed disenfranchisement by means of a poor general education. Whether a school is religious or secular, public or private, chartered or online, or homeschool, it is fundamentally critical to have a pragmatic curricular science with superior and involved teachers who can meet rigorous standards of spiritual and intellectual achievement.

Learning

As studies in brain function progressed, various areas of soft neurological signs were identified in the different cortexes that related to receptive and expressive capabilities and capacities. These findings demonstrated the functional complexities of the human brain. Diagnosis is an involved process, requiring many professionals, and care must be taken not to label people in narrow ways. There are many facets of *intelligence* (the scholastic definition) and we can't measure every type. (*Oxford Unabridged Dict., 41, 1989*) A high scholastic intelligence does not always equate with understanding. Understanding is finding *useful* relationships per one's intelligence. This results in creative (as opposed to destructive) end-results. "Usefulness" here would imply the considerate inclusion of components involving ethics and morality...the foundation for developing virtue.

I identify seven levels of learning from my dictionary studies...(1) sensation, (2) raw data, (3) information, (4) knowledge, (5) intelligence, (6) understanding, and (7) wisdom. Sensation becomes raw data when the individual *notes* some manifestation of space/time/matter/energy/mind as meaning something. In turn, that data becomes information when it is categorized and catalogued with previously acquired information (related data), then retained in a mental database. This retention leads to acquiring fields of knowledge comprising one's *general knowledge*. one may assume the more fields of knowledge, and the breadth and depth of those fields, the greater the resulting working intelligence. However, one's *academic* intelligence can be lacking in qualitative aspects, for example, the absence of emotional intelligence.

General knowledge is the basis for *daily problem solving*. Intelligence is the quantitative and qualitative use of one's general knowledge. With working intelligence we achieve *understanding*. However, understanding alone can't resolve many circumstances. *Wisdom* is the highest level of learning. It is the ability to appropriately *apply justice and mercy* actively from understanding. Wisdom is essential and key to overcoming personal and social extremism. Some people may have a relatively small accumulation of general intelligence. They may not have a lot of book learning, a high I. Q., or even much in the way of "street smarts", yet they are wise. This is because the intelligence they possess has *integrity*. Tempered with virtue, these people act in beneficial ways. Wisdom and virtue go hand in hand.

Competence in Self-Perspective

One ought to ignore those who refuse to elevate their level of discourse beyond bias, derogatory language, exaggeration, and unfounded accusation. This is easier said than done. Many in the adult world are failing. Yet, those who are observant…will recognize life's intricate nature and learn a certain respect and reverence for humanity's complexity. There are those who do not feel bound to peer review or rational self-evaluation who become a source for extreme ideology. As evidenced by the history of world wars...victorious supremacists or other narcissistic extremists of any kind, would annihilate, imprison or enslave anyone not fitting their perverse description of what it means to be a "perfect", or the "right kind" of human being.

If it were not one kind of difference, such as skin color, it would be something else. Personal problem resolution is not relevant to these people...and ongoing blame and vengeance becomes its own purpose. Social extremism is about character flaws such as selfishness, personal insecurity, vengeful anger, loss of self-control, and craving power over others. Unchecked by the awareness and virtues of a given populace, such extremism spreads like a wildfire of spiritual cancer.

Chapter 7

History: A Broken Time Capsule

History and Interpretation

Recorded history accounts for only a microscopic portion of the human experience. Historians, anthropologists, archaeologists, geneticists, linguists and other disciplines of hard and soft science have attempted to piece together a basic chronology of various social and geopolitical timelines. Ancient populations and their cities or villages were built near pre-existing and current water sources, therefore, many records and artifacts lie underneath our present-day cities and sunken under seas and oceans...which leaves much of it politically, religiously or pragmatically impossible to excavate. There is, therefore, a vast number of unaccounted for records, artifacts, and historic structures...far beyond what we have unearthed.

Historic material is exposed to the elements, continental drift, meteorological and cosmological events...as the impacts of time and motion take their toll. This reality of historical vacuums, unfortunately, does not stop some from filling in and fabricating history...to fit a preferred personal view. Isolated individuals and ideological groups, who do not feel ethically bound to professional peer review or reasonable self-evaluation, produce mostly distorted research and literature. Such becomes crude sources of misinformation...often encouraging irrational antipathies, misanthropy, and extremism.

History and Academia

In the broadest sense, human history is an ongoing series of innumerable events involving people and their external environment. It is the essence of our existence to create and experience events. All societies and their manner of development are built around such events as exploration, discovery, invention, innovation, agriculture of land and water, industry, natural and man-made disasters, war, treaties, trade, commerce, genealogies, music, art, dance, sports, traditions, worship, celebrations, rituals and other natural, man-made, and cosmic phenomena. These events lead to the creation of complex social structures and build, change, or destroy secular and religious institutions over time. History records extensive human tragedy attributed to a desire for power and control, with governments often holding attitudes of superiority. One reason to study history is to understand the genesis or motivations behind human behavior. For example, by observing current events and researching historical events, one may find parallels as to how events started, what transpired, and why the actors on all sides took the actions they did. However, certain rogue researchers may insist everyone accept their given perspective and attitude regarding historical events. Nevertheless, forcing conclusions out of historical deficits or contrived contexts is unwarranted and may inadvertently lead to condoning extreme perspectives.

One should also keep in mind that guesstimates on regional boundaries and timelines, encapsulated cultural information, subjective interpretations by historians, legend, myth, and extrapolations on scientific research by the overly enthusiastic, all add to the confusion and difficulty of examining the recorded past. Yet, one thing seems certain from historical recordings...history is full of extreme instances in human behavior and strange phenomena. As such, historians with various interpretations of the world's social and political history can find and point to bizarre and isolated anecdotal examples in records and in anthropological evidence, and then paint a broad picture of their findings using a limited spectrum of criteria that will support their particular version of existence. This is why people find historical accuracy easy to question.

Limits of Ancient Records Acquisition

In the last few hundred years, archaeology, (which is limited to relatively small, low-populated, and unrestricted sites), has unearthed but a minute fraction (or tip) of an incomprehensibly massive iceberg of all human civilization. One need only examine satellite imagery to understand how expansive the earth's surface is, and the extent to which vast areas of land are presently unoccupied by humans...including sunken masses under the ocean.

Finding portions of ancient artifacts through ground work is hardly representative of the vastness of lost civilizations, large and small. Due to natural barriers, geopolitical interests, territorial security complexities and local beliefs and heritage...accessibility to localities and regions is more difficult and risky than one could imagine. The point being that, whatever humans thought and did throughout history infinitely outweighs what we have in reliable records or evidentiary material.

If we get into the specifics of exact time lines and interpretation of events, it becomes highly subjective as one expert says this...and another says that. Sometimes different views complement each other and sometimes they contradict. Although we ought to study history from different recognized and respected authorities, there is no excuse to start making up history just to complete one's own preferred historical narrative. Unfortunately, self-noted or self-proclaimed historians allow considerable emotional and intellectual bias into their interpretations. As with any objective studies or research, personal virtue is crucial.

Addressing Historical Revisionism

Almost all historical research has some revisionism. For the most part, it is impossible to avoid. *American Imperialism* is a favorite phrase amongst socialists. Few take the time to look up and examine the meaning of the word "imperialism". Only its negative connotation of force or threat of force is acceptable to socialists. That is amazingly hypocritical since socialism is historically associated strongly with a violent and forceful imperialism. In its best sense, imperialism is diplomatically sharing what one believes is a better way. It is not by force, but by mutual agreement between peaceful nations. If a nation is hostile to other nations, then diplomacy is still sought...however, this will necessarily change the nature of the diplomacy. A cut and dried use of the word "imperialism", to be fair, is hardly representative of the various complex contexts of world affairs. (Although imperialism was typical in history, it is not practiced by America in that sense today)

There is also a difference between the words colonization and colonialism. The latter implies a forceful element that the former does not. As the world became more regionally connected, complexities in international relations increased. In the global era, isolationism proved unfeasible and dangerous. Some history is "hot button" sensitive. Today, there are frequent references to the injustices done to Native Americans and the South's inception of African Slavery. Anyone with any common sense realizes these injustices happened...as did the Holocaust. Such horrors have been perpetuated throughout human history...as far back as one can go. Sometimes war is necessary to stop these injustices. Sometimes war is just war between equally guilty parties.

We could blame all Germans for WWI. We did that...with a vengeance...and the repercussions to the German population, implemented by a world council, were so severe...they had nowhere to turn except Hitler...leading to even greater devastation in WWII. Some Christians blame the Jews for the crucifixion of Christ...which is disingenuous, since it was the so-called spiritual leaders, lawyers, scribes and other elite at the time involved. Jews were the first Christians, and the wider populace of Jews had nothing to do with it. Besides...knowing Christian doctrine...someone had to do it. Christ forgave the Roman Soldiers...because they did not understand. (*Luke 23:34*) That is an example to follow.

In addressing slavery, more Americans lost their lives in the American Civil War than any war before or since. It doesn't mean slavery was the reason for every individual on either side of the conflict. Greed, confusion, and sloth played into it beyond racism. There were a few thousand known black owners of slaves. African tribes helped enslave other tribes. Native Americans are known to have had thousands of black slaves. (*Snopes, 42, 2019*) In any case, inadequacies abound in the misrepresentations of events in their various historical and situational contexts...often misplacing blame and ignoring the cultural era and complexities in accountability.

Regarding early America, native tribes often welcomed the colonists and valued their trade. Some were peaceful and did not feel threatened by immigrants looking for a place to live free. Others were threatened by outsiders, but realized their intentions were not evil (In most cases). Yet other tribes were violent by nature, even to other tribes. As well, Native American ancestors are believed to be ancient migrants from the Asiatic regions...including Siberia. In the end, most of the devastation...unfortunate and unknown to the populace at the time...was the transmission of disease from Europe. It was not done purposefully. (*Wikipedia, 43, undated*) Did the U.S. Army eventually force Native

Americans onto reservations? Yes...distrust, land development, and space had become issues. Was it wrong? Yes. There is no excuse. Reparations have been made in various instances and is ongoing today (*U.S. Gov., 44, 2016*) Sovereignties have also been granted. (*Wikipedia, 45, 2018*)

There are always instances anecdotal to the general flow of historical events. America, like any other nation has made some gross errors and missteps. Those errors and missteps are the focus of critics who would paint a severe picture of America. The overall reality is something different. World historian Anthony Pagden asks is the United States really an empire? "I think if we look at the history of the European empires, the answer must be no. It is often assumed that because America possesses the military capability to become an empire, any overseas interest it does have must necessarily be imperial....In a number of crucial respects, the United States is, indeed, very un-imperial.... America bears not the slightest resemblance to ancient Rome. Unlike all previous European empires, it has no significant overseas settler populations in any of its formal dependencies and no obvious desire to acquire any....It exercises no direct rule anywhere outside these areas, and it has always attempted to extricate itself as swiftly as possible from anything that looks as if it were about to develop into direct rule." (*Wikidepia.org/American Imperialism*)

Nevertheless, the idea that a land is eternally owned by a "given" people is pragmatically untenable. Reality dictates that genealogies and civilizations are fluid in time and motion. Laws should be established by any fair-minded people governing *temporal* property rights. However... all mortal life is temporary, and one's location is arbitrary on this planet. We are born into the world by happenstance. Populations grow diversely at different rates and land has to be used by "someone else" eventually. Adaptation is not always smooth. Imminent domain and manifest destiny are often abused, yet are viable concepts within certain contexts. There is no doubt...many seeking power, wealth and control are guilty of great atrocities...from most every culture, ethnic, and race. Yet, cooperation for space is a necessary negotiation when populations grow. Although I am personally not against new reparations, it sets an impossible precedent. As well, those who would consider socialism as a form of reparation could only make it worse.

I am not being flippant or insensitive. Without understanding history in a practical sense...fear and suspicion will get the best of some people and groups. Conspiracies do exist, but not around every corner with everyday people. The phrase "Social Justice Warriors" often alludes to those immature personalities who see themselves as being "outside" of the human equation, above the fray, and not contributing to the woes of the world. However, we all contribute...because we are all here and imperfect. The answers never did lie in finding causes for historical blaming. Nevertheless, a virtuous society must demand justice regarding those who practice racism today, as well as those who engage in modern-day slavery.

Chapter 8

Law and Disorder

The Great Charter of the Liberties

In the United States the law is designed to protect the liberty of the individual citizen. A prelude and forerunner to the Bill of Rights was the *Magna Carta*. It was a document "signed by King John after negotiations with his barons and their French and Scots allies at Runnymede, Surrey, England in 1215. It is one of the most celebrated documents in the History of England. It is recognised as a cornerstone of the idea of the liberty of citizens." Another related concept of individual liberty that predated the Magna Carter (although not made law until 1679) was *Habeas Corpus*. It is a Latin phrase meaning "produce the body." By means of the writ of habeas corpus a court may order the state to "produce the body," or hand over a prisoner so that it might review the legality of the prisoner's detention. (*Wikipedia, 46, undated*)

What is Law?

Law is the development of systems of logic created to reason out and support a position. (*The Oxford English Dictionary, 47, 1989*) Law creates order. The U.S. Constitution is our preeminent law, and martial law it's only exception. When we examine the history of American law, what large corporation doesn't employ a division of lawyers? Why? The U.S. government, state governments, and lower governments use agency regulatory codes, numbered in the hundreds of thousands, and also an intricate judicial system to regulate and enforce laws governing the many aspects of American public and private life. Military law is outside of this.

There are some fifty-plus areas of national life covered in the U.S. Code that are regulated by four hundred-plus agencies and sub-agencies at the federal level. Just the federal tax code alone is currently over four thousand pages long. Corporate lawyers are needed to both understand endless business, health, safety, tax, and other codes at international, federal, state, county, and municipal levels...and to combat lawsuits from the general public, other private entities, as well as the government. It is complex, however, despite the reputation attributed to its profession, beyond creating order, law also creates jobs and prevents war.

Questionable Legal Practices

Law is the most powerful of academic studies when it comes to influencing the direction American society takes. The U.S. Congress is full of lawyers who create federal laws under the auspices of our constitutional law. In courts, along with ascertaining lies, noting discrepancies, and citing logic errors in the opposition, lawyers also use case-law precedent and a legal nomenclature with a complex jargon (legalese) to reason in favor of an argument. Be forewarned, legalese is not Standard English. There has been a push in the recent past to require "normal" language in legal and contractual documentation. (*Benson, 48, 1985*) Along with this coded vocabulary, the most effective courtroom lawyers are very much aware of human conceptualization weaknesses when it comes to cognition and memory, and the resulting possibility for people to equivocate or extrapolate under emotional stress. Therein lies one strategy to discredit witnesses.

As I implicated previously, history is impossible to recreate with precision, and well-trained lawyers are very much aware of this. To put the situation of a criminal courtroom into better perspective...let us say a very rich person is on trial for murder and is pleading insanity. The financial resources of the rich person allow him or her to find a top-flight lawyer and defense team that will search the nation over for the best available psychologists and psychiatrists to support the defendant's claim of insanity. The team will have numerous well-paid paralegals to quickly search through the thousands of cases in private legal databases, including public and proprietary databases such as *LexisNexis* and *West-Law*, to find precedents that may support the defendant's case. The rich person on trial is also more likely to have friends and connections in high places, and the wherewithal to monitor the entire legal process to catch the prosecution in a technical error.

Here's the opposition. The prosecution is funded by the city/area of jurisdiction, has a limited budget, and will have to rely upon the knowledge and savvy of their prosecutor (often an Assistant District Attorney), with maybe a couple of so-so-paid paralegal assistants. Regardless of the specifics of the case, the rich person has a much better chance of winning, getting off, or at least bargaining a lesser sentence than a poor person in the same situation. Are rich and poor equal under the law? The laws are in the books for all...but being able to use them, knowing about them, enforcing them...these are separate considerations.

The Science of Logic

In our criminal and civil courts lawyers and judges decide results. While scientific experts asked to testify may value heuristics (experimentation, trial and error, etc.), if there are any weaknesses in a courtroom presentation, lawyers are capable of shredding such methods to pieces with the rules of logic...which is also a field of science. While scientists and engineers usually put complex things together, lawyers routinely take them apart. Lawyers can easily exploit those who are not skilled in logic. As we all know, it is always easier to take something apart then to put it together. With logic, the quality and complexity of our memory patterns depend in great measure on the level of cognitive competence one exercises in processing information from the environment. Therefore, it is easy for legal experts to question one's mental processing.

Humans use association, contrast, inference, deduction, induction, analysis, synthesis, observation, inquiry, theory, hypothesizing, postulation, experimentation, cause and effect, abstraction, and so forth when formulating ideas and conclusions. We can see there is plenty of mental territory for a lawyer to find fault in human reasoning. If you are so inclined, you can look up hundreds of "logic errors" on the Internet, which courtroom lawyers memorize. The fact is...the concepts or experiences we retain in memory can be based on external realities, our imagination and emotion, or a mix. I believe the best protection from law is personal virtue.

Lawlessness of Anarchy

Anarchy is defined as "a state of disorder due to absence or non recognition of authority". (*Google Dictionary, 49, undated*) This something many supremacists, communists, and isolated militias support...to affect changes without regard to general society. KKK, Nazi supremacist groups, and Communist ANTIFA are good examples...whether they know it or not. There are also some who are personally frustrated with the inadequate resource distribution and social complexities created by massive populations, such that they might support the idea of anarchy. The problem with anarchy is that, as a general rule, a lot of babies get thrown out with the bath water. Some people don't have a problem with anarchy so long as the ones getting killed by it are not themselves. Despite problems with some authorities, chaos won't lead to order.

The reality is life becomes highly complex with any form of government of a large population, especially if the people themselves are not peaceful, productive, and resourceful. Lawless anarchists, like other extremists, usually have no intention of getting along with anyone. The pretense of using violence, chaos, with survivalism to achieve a natural order, is as flawed as history itself. It's been tried with horrifying results throughout history. Like religious, ethnic and environmental extremisms, any social extremism such as anarchy is essentially a declaration of war against systems in general, and against anyone who does not agree with their radicalism and do as they say.

Chapter 9

Politics of Faith and Fear

The Eternal Sea

During the spring of 1977 my cousin and I were coming back to Oregon from a road trip to Yellowstone. Due to several hundred miles worth of wrong turns we ended up lost for about 2 days in the upper mountains of Idaho. As we came to one dead end, there was a man walking out from a wood lodge. If I recall correctly, he had a gun at his side. As we explained our situation he invited us to come in. Thinking quickly, we thanked him profusely and said we must be on our way. As we drove away I breathed a sigh of relief. I did not know much about supremacists back then, but I think we both sensed the danger. In honest reflection, I think if our skin had been of a different color, we might not be here today.

Even in a free and lawful society, there is no guarantee of safety from the acts of others. Even so, our chances for a good quality of life are much better if we do live in such a society. As citizens we have a duty to insure that society is safe and free for all. That includes the duty to vote for virtuous people to hold the power in maintaining our laws and freedoms. Some have referred to politics as the eternal sea. It is forever ongoing and so must be our vigilance in maintaining a good society. That we vote…and who we vote for…does have eternal significance. If one votes for what one thinks is right and good, that is enough, regardless of others opinions.

Politics Defined

Politics is the art and science of the governance of a state. A state is a self-governing political community occupying its own territory. (*Free Online Dictionary, 50, undated*) Because each individual in a state has differences in political thought…diplomacy, statesmanship, negotiation, delegation, and compromise are skills essential to effective politics. Understanding of the law can bring great power and control in politics, either to help or destroy individuals…and society. Regarding politicians, one should beware of those who seek desperately to hold on to the "old boys club", or perhaps the "new girls club", of privilege and assumed superiority.

For instance, term limits in U.S. congressional politics is essential to restraining fiscal extremes in both the over-taxing and the continuing frivolous "pork barrel" expenditures at the federal and state level. Congressional politicians are motivated to keep their "golden ticket" jobs as permanent fixtures by appeasing the special interests of their state through the funding of targeted projects, which entities, in turn, find ways to reward the politician. This is neither a service to the national public, nor an intended function of the federal government. A *Convention of the States* is the only alternative to remove this "staying" power from Congress, unless most of Congress suddenly becomes virtuous and passes a bill.

Organizations are Inevitable

Social and technological development in mass populations portends the creation of (or continuation of) esoteric (non-mainstream) religious and

secular associations and entities such as secret societies or cabals...
frequently developing out of the major and minor secular and/or reli-
gious/philosophical practices and institutions of the day. Some are con-
tinuous from the ancient past. Some of these organizations most likely
have past technologies and information unknown to the mainstream.
For example, existing trade secrets, inventions and methods are not just
those registered with a government patent office. Many stereotype
them all as cults. However, the term "cult" has been applied broadly to
so many organizations, and from so many varied sources, that this term
has been rendered meaningless.

Some organizations are essentially beneficial and cooperative in nature,
having a sincere intent to provide service and to find answers to the evil
that people do. Other such organizations which trend more towards
extreme sentiment and actions may precipitate the eventual corruption,
devolution, and destruction of an established social order, along with
its useful structures. Others yet, are straightforward criminal in nature.
Successful organizations exist and survive for a reason. Often one can
find the reason(s) through personal secondary research. However, if
one finds that the entity they are researching is bent upon evil intents
and behavior to accomplish its goals, this entails a risk to the researcher.
There are safe ways to investigate and analyze an organization from
afar. Then one can anonymously (safely) report anything substantial to
the proper authorities.

Extreme Organizations
One observable characteristic of an extreme organization is the existence of a program of subversive indoctrination (meant to undermine current social authorities and governing systems) The primary
purpose of such programs is to isolate the individual from his or
her former social relations. Controlling another's personal
anonymy and autonomy is a psychological and physical captivity.

This approach, following recruitment, can create an atmosphere in which to implant a highly exclusive, cliquish, dysfunctional, and dependent "group" mentality.

This gives the controller(s) power. These are the conditions that will typically lead to memory manipulation, emotional coaching, and ultimately a psychological "clearing" for re-education. This is brainwashing. Once a sense of total investment (emotional and financial) is achieved in a particular person, force by fear of harm (real or imagined) becomes an effective tactic to counteract any internal revolts, and thus, foils any outside attempts to intervene, deprogram, or mainstream a susceptible individual back to a balanced social-emotional health.

Over time, the attention a disturbed extremist leader receives, and the belongingness the followers feel, become a reciprocal reinforcement that can create a powerfully addictive and symbiotically extreme, dysfunctional codependency. If a leader becomes psychotic...delusional thinking and hallucinatory experiences may start to play into bizarre, criminal, or self-destructive activities. Individuals in these extreme organizations may experience changes from previously healthy behaviors, to disturbing and dangerous behaviors.

Wilcox identifies common behaviors prevalent in the communication and actions of extremists. These include character assassination instead of addressing an issue; sweeping generalizations without evidence; selectivity in facts...exaggerating similarities and ignoring contradictions; double standards in excusing one's own acts while emphasizing good intentions, and doing just the opposite when critical of the acts of others. (*L. Wilcox, 51, 2017*) Unfortunately, this is what we see in the characters of many of those leading discussions on major news channels and talk shows. There is nothing virtuous to be found in such characters.

Chapter 10

Free Will and Extremism

Choice and the Origins of Extremism

Normal functioning individuals can stop…and think…to consider the consequences of an action they take, or they can react impulsively, indifferently and thoughtlessly. If one acknowledges one could go either way, it should be self-evident that one possesses the ability to choose. How and why do people choose to do bad things? Unless there is some psycho-physiological dysfunction, such as insanity, or similar trauma…a criminally inclined personality or character, as I define it…does not just happen. It takes a series of bad decisions over time…crossing over safe boundaries, ignoring natural inhibitions, and breaking healthy social mores. For example, those individuals who are impatient and act to exercise unearned authorities, controls, and powers…not granted by common consent…are making choices that ultimately become a threat to themselves and to society.

Most people come to realize that a healthy balance and effort in diet, sleep, thinking, feeling, learning, exercising, working, socializing, recreating, interacting in various settings, etc. is key to healthy functioning. Good habits developed over time are essential. I also believe characteristics like gratitude and humility are essential to health and happiness. On the other hand, personal neglect in these areas can lead to social emotional extremes in thoughts and behaviors, and are bound to be manifested in future expressions and acts.

An example of imbalance and neglect in youth might be idle thoughts, laziness, and persistently useless inactivity such as lottering. Poor habits of this nature can ultimately disenfranchise an individual from the expectations and requirements of a given society. Another might be an overly intense, unregulated, and isolated intellectual or religious pursuit of an individual, which can outpace his or her own mental, emotional, and spiritual capacity. As a result, dysfunctional thinking and behavior patterns can translate to irrational attitudes and expectations, poor decision-making and antisocial behavior. These are irresponsible ways of thinking and doing that is characteristic of social extremism.

Extremes in Science

My purpose is to give context to mitigate misconceptions regarding some people's interpretations of science. "Logy" (ology) pertains to a field of scientific study and denotes a body of principles, theories, data, etc., produced by learned endeavor (*Wiktionary, 52, undated*). Due to the inherent subjectivity of humans, it can be very difficult to obtain a relevant degree of objectivity and reliability in any field of science. Conclusions are usually argued among scientists who gathered the hard data. There are theories of space, matter, motion, time, and mind...which always prove vastly incomplete...or simply wrong.

There are also differences in defining what is a hard or soft science. Most country's science academies have significant differences in their categorization and the number of sciences. The idea of a "settled science" in any of these fields suggest a finality that doesn't exist. The limits in human sensations of sight, sound, touch, kinesthetics, and olfactory abilities, even when assisted by advanced instrumentations and technologies, means we cannot presently observe the greater part of the micro and macro universe. Nor can we directly observe the past, even with atomic-deterioration technology.

Consider also that a reliable objectivity is simply not possible with some personalities. An age-old temptation for many scientists (and religionists as well), is to ultimately say and do what others want them to say and do, and they will presently be rewarded. Some in science base their self-worth on group status and stature. When a field of study has fair evidence that puts the traditional view in question, the status quo quickly mobilizes to suppress and marginalize findings and discoveries that provide an alternate logic. If one is not careful to balance an involved thinking process with fairness and other considerations, obsession can creep into a narrow crevice of intellectual extremism. (*Office of Research Integrity [ORI], 53, undated*) One need only examine the history of criminally deranged war-time scientists and their activities to understand the horrors associated with an indifferent, inhumane science.

This does not mean we ignore science. Most agree that pure science is cool and wonderful. It is part of us and our learning. It's not a secular "possession". Nevertheless, in the world of theoretical research, some scientists attempt analysis and conclusions that are beyond them. There may be approaches seeking a separation of cognition and emotion, the elemental and the composite, the physical and the metaphysical. Certainly analysis has its applications, however, unless one is a hundred percent psychopathic, for example, a complete dichotomy of cognition and emotion...to attain a so-called pure objectivity...is not achievable (or advisable) for a normal person.

There is nothing in the fundamental definition of science that precludes the metaphysical. On the contrary, rather science is one aspect of human inquiry that opens itself to all possibilities...the seen (e.g., atomic explosions) and the unseen (e.g., dark matter)...or so they say. As well, science facts are subject to review and change, especially with a shift in paradigm. (*Shuttleworth, 54, 2008*) The word "science", like philosophy or religion, is merely a neutral term that addresses an aspect of our active intelligent being. Neither science nor religion is evil. Hence to say that science or religion creates war is meaningless. To say people misuse and abuse science and religion to create war has substance.

Extremes in Religion

With some Faiths, no one is certain what their intentions are because the members are elusive and not given to open discussion of their religion with others. Such groups may discourage investigation by well-meaning visitors. Although sacredness is a valid reason to be cautious, yet, without some open-door policy, it is impossible for others to evaluate and access a belief system. Some may start to assume the religion in question is covert in nature, and that deception towards "outsiders" is acceptable and encouraged. Such behaviors by members may lead to the practice of condescension, or perhaps rationalizing deception towards "unbelievers".

Elusive responses to sincere questions can raise suspicions as to the motivations and intents of a Faith's teachings. It is certainly okay for people of faith to say "I don't know". However, some religious groups may employ an absolutist approach, requiring a strict obedience without censure of the reasons behind certain principles or acts. The universal religious ideals of brotherly love, helping those in need, sharing substance with others, free will and so forth, reflect the opposite of force and fear. Surely God has given us a brain to think and emotions to feel. Most mainstream faiths I am aware of practice moderation and balance that emphasizes a healthy personal spirituality over an oppressive fundamentalism.

Fundamentalism is not Spirituality

Fundamentalism (referring to the general word-meaning and *not* the specific historical movements) is actually the opposite of spirituality, wherein fear, force, and a strict orthodox...perhaps militant...adherence to tradition (as opposed to a personally chosen obedience to certain principles) are the operating controllers. (*Oxford Dictionaries, 55, 2013*) With spirituality (not to be confused with Spiritualism) faith, hope, charity and love, are primary examples of the operating motivators to encourage people through personal choice to obey a Faith's perception of God or providence.

Fundamentalists may habitually take their faith's *own* scriptural passages out of the various spiritual, historical and cultural contexts germane to its proper comprehension...as it was intended by the original author(s). As history shows repeatedly, this leads to practices by certain fundamentalist groups that are absent of any moral responsibility and consideration to fellow humans. This is just another form of extremism. Some of these religious groups may even feel revenge is justified in scripture by circumstance. Revenge is never justified in pure Christianity...as it would also justify hatred.

Mainstream religions should value life, liberty and self-preservation. Many extreme ideologues believe in a self-serving martyrdom and taking as many other innocent souls into the "next life" with them as possible. This destruction of life is valued more to such people than the creation of life given to us by God. I know of no scripture of any major religion, which suggests we should not be thankful to God for the lives we are given. Those who see differently are undoubtedly operating lives of desperation, anger, and willful ignorance.

Although we in Christianity are advised to be "harmless as doves", in like manner we are advised to be "wise as serpents". Having true faith is to be spiritually guided, not blind or naïve. Certain dysfunctional and disenfranchised associations may reciprocate emotions and actions and thereby reinforce extremes in thought and behavior. These groups or organizations, much like the individual, as previously stated, are typically inconsiderate and indifferent to what "outsiders" might be thinking or feeling. This is a social condition for spawning hatred and hate groups. Virtue cannot survive in such an environment.

As I previously stressed, extremism in thought, expression, and action which is rationalized and justified, ultimately leads to racism, fundamentalism, anti-religious and anti-secular intolerances, discrimination, criminal organization, violent gangs, terrorism, ethnic cleansing, anarchy, war crimes, holocausts, and a host of other social ills and evils. Social extremes is a symptom of one seeking a shortcut and an avoidance of life's more difficult personal challenges.

The Roots of Terrorism

Following this book's train of thought...I would suggest that (1) an antisocial personality, (2) an economic/educational/social disenfranchisement, (3) a fundamentalist mentality, (4) early abuse and trauma, or various combinations of these...are all possible sources of terrorism. Terrorism can happen in highly organized political, business, humanitarian, and religious settings...which are often used as "fronts" for an agenda. There are personalities that will cloak themselves as "martyrs for a cause" through a charity...whether it is for attacking other religions...or perhaps attacking social infrastructure in the guise of protecting the environment, "God's honor", a disenfranchised people, etc., from a real or supposed government enemy.

Terrorism can give a purpose....a cause...a recognition...to those who are lost, despondent, or bent upon vengeance. It doesn't matter so much to these confused people where they find their designated targets, so long as it results in some kind of destructive outlet and mass attention to appease their misguided motives and frustration. As is usually the case for those who cross a psychological and physical line into persistent violent thinking and behavior, there is an accompanying transference from a feeling of personal failure to blaming another person, a specific organization, or a faceless society for this failure.

Freedom and Free will

Free will and emotions are the principal aspects of consciousness and conscience that make us sentient beings, and self-aware humans. Without them, we are puppets of a universe and history already decided, and our fates are ultimately as predictable as night follows day. Those who do not believe free will exist are apparently capable of denying the reality of human unpredictability in everyday life. Free will is independent of the determinants of nature and nurture and creates this unpredictability. This should become more apparent when those with similar backgrounds and genetic attributes...choose entirely different life paths.

One should also be aware that freedom and free will are different concepts. Our freedoms can be limited in a number of ways. We may have sensory, mental, or physical disabilities. Geopolitical boundaries may be imposed upon us. Laws may impose legal consequences on us. We must have air to breathe and water to drink from the earth. Such temporal limits determine the breadth of one's external physical freedoms. On the other hand, free will is an internal volition...and grants one personal agency, and we decide how we will respond within the freedoms or boundaries that society and nature presently provide...or impose on us. No one can influence our free will without our acquiescence.

Nature, Nurture and Free Will

At first glance, it appears that genetic and social influences dictate human behavior. This perspective reasons that by having such power over human behavior, social problems may naturally dissolve. However, we must recognize that there exists a third influence upon the individual that is independent from nurturing (environment/external nature) and natural (genetic/internal nature) influences. This third influence, *free will*, cannot be found within our genetic code or through a scientific investigation. It cannot be isolated by scientific method, imposed on us, or taken from us by others. However, we can observe its operation in our external environment, and experience it within ourselves.

Free will becomes evident when choices are presented or made, but we are not compelled to select an option, or act on it, simply because it exists. While it cannot be denied that social and genetic influences (determinants) are indispensable tools to the fashioning of our attributes, it is anticipated that these influences teach us *how* we can resolve social and psychological problems...but only the influence of free will allows us to *act* upon those teachings.

Once we understand that free will dictates the ultimate decisions in all things, we begin to feel the weight of personal responsibility not found in the usual study of social psychology and human genetics. We cannot always help what we are, what we think, or how we feel, but we can recognize that we have options in choosing how to respond or deal with a situation, thus re-influencing our own thoughts, feelings, and actions. This acceptance of personal responsibility empowers one to seek insight, find solutions, or attempt actions not otherwise considered.

This being the case, how might I define the work of those who engage in endless, fixated, pedantic writing about socialism? Volumes of boring...often disjointed writing, even with fancy vocabulary, does not make one smarter that others. Logic errors are prevalent throughout their thinking. Individualism, for example, is not adverse to community, cooperation, and association. Rather it is complementary to it. Some are constantly trying to make society "right", assuming there is a problem or contradiction where none exist. They also ignore the state of those countries who practice(d) it. Perhaps they are too busy trying to fix other people and society and ignoring their own personal shortcomings? Instead, perhaps one should get a practical job and become part of an already functional society?

Rather than busily pointing out all of life's supposed shortcomings, perhaps they fail to recognize that the egalitarian paradise they seek already exist around them in America. It may already exist within those who have mastered themselves. It does, however, require some education and applying oneself. If one doesn't make this effort, is there to be no consequence for this personal failure? If a person drinks irresponsibly...if they take illegal or harmful drugs...if they constantly fight others...if they engage in criminal activity and make no effort to succeed in anything in any way...are we supposed to prop up this individual and provide them equality in wealth, marriage, family, possessions, etc.? These things require personal effort and wisdom. Should we forget about that? Socialism is a dead philosophy...let it rest in peace.

Epilogue

There is a fundamental concept that lies at the heart of many philosophical discussions. It is the ideal of "evil". Does it exist? I say yes...and I say also...so does good. The best general definition of evil I can give is...it is that which destroys people at their core. People naturally seek to be truly happy with themselves and their purposes. Whatever destroys this personal happiness and purpose, we can call it evil. True happiness comes from the essence of a good character. We can feel good about ourselves in spite of the harsh realities that may surround us. Whatever destroys our character, will destroy us...our purposes and our happiness.

There exists no set of ideas or group of books which resolves the problem of evil. Evil is not resolvable. It exist because good exist, and vice versa. Good and evil exist through choice. When we continually choose against our conscience, we start to lose our sense of right and wrong. This impacts one's character. Extremisms more easily creep in. By seeking what is virtuous...one can avoid this pitfall. Religious, quasi-religious, or even secular organizations, including some calling themselves satanic, could be microsisms of a much larger, global-wide symbiotic dysfunctional codependency system...like that of corporatism with its narcissists (the controllers), and socialism with its passivists (the controlled).

Some free thinkers are known to write what is referred to as "fringe esoterica". There is a lot of reification in this writing. The word reify (using the *fallacy* definition) refers to treating any mental abstraction the same as if it were actual or concrete existence. (*Wikipedia, 56, 2013*) However, their written product is often nothing more than a pretense for substance…a form of illusory mysticism and whimsical extrapolation banking on borrowed time. Stephen R. Covey writes that in the last half-century or so, that there has been a significant change in emphasis in social psychology from internal character development to acquiring a superficial or *surface* personality. (*Covey, 57, 2004*) Appearances have their place, but it never substitutes for character.

New theories and philosophies, which amount to pop-psychology, are taught in many universities across the nation. The new attitudes accompany a reluctance to accept accountability in moral and ethical matters that directly address personal character. Often, psychology taught in college classes is now used more to manipulate the public than actually benefit them. There is also an attempt to make all ethical and moral matters relative to the point of anything you do or say is okay…if you can articulate a rational. Nothing could be further from the truth. What good we do in our immediate surroundings…in our relationships where we have some control…is most important. Virtue should always be our guide.

An unfortunate consequence of this misguided emphasis in universities regarding these "poly jargonic elucidations" in personality and purpose, is that now many antisocial personalities have developed much better skills in deception and manipulation. By focusing on just the outward signs of normalcy and an apparent "cool" personality…these alone, are mistakenly interpreted as signs of good mental and emotional health. Today…many more of these charismatic people can insidiously incorporate themselves into every facet of political, economic, and domestic life without getting the needed mental healthcare. Their impact on society is devastating.

Society at large is no longer sensitive to what really constitutes good or bad character in individuals. We are therefore "shocked" with unforeseen events of terror, criminality, and political turmoil...in what otherwise was considered a peaceful and innocent setting. Finding a healthy balance in self requires mental, spiritual, and physical effort. One cannot "wing it" on the most important matters of life. From my experience, a sincere look inward and towards the eternal, is a step in the right direction, and towards virtue.

Appendix

Researching Socialism:

The following review includes an expanded talk, a manifesto, and 3 books...these 5 sources include two modern proponents of socialism (Ray Nunes and Michael Newman), a primary source of socialism (The Communist Manifesto), and two opponents of socialism...one current and one from the mid 20th century (Kristian Niemietz and Ludwig Von Mises). I maintain there is really nothing much good about the economic philosophy of socialism beyond its dreamy desired end result. Many of those who attempt to rationalize its modern failures are pedantic in their obfuscations, equivocate on word meanings, and divert from the subject at hand with an overload of tangents and irrelevant citations, apparently trying to get across to everyone that socialism, when it works, is way too complex for the average person to understand. Apparently it is also too complex for its supporters to articulate and put in understandable words, why it is better than capitalism.

What is Socialism?
Ray Nunes
Former Chairman of Workers Party of New Zealand
(A Talk Given to Students)
https://www.marxists.org/history/erol/new-zealand/nunes-socialism.pdf

Ray Nunes was a theorist who devoted much of his life to analyzing communism. He believed practical revisionisms corrupted socialism's true form. His studies included the original 19th century Utopians, French men Charles Fourier and Henri Saint-Simon, and also Englishman Robert Owen. Rooted in the current social conditions of WWII coming out of feudalism "into the throes of the industrial revolution", Nunes developed a sympathy for the oppressed of the working class. He believed Marx developed socialism into a science with the development of dialectical materialism (the idea that things create thought, as opposed to thought creating things) People were, therefore, reactionary more than actionable. In reality, things and thoughts are inextricably bound to each other and people are both, so I consider this a flawed, unidimensional idea by Marx.

This idea, combined with Marx's political philosophy and his theory of class struggle, apparently composes a "real science" that the working class can use against the enemy capitalists. Nunes explains that in Marxist philosophy, the "mode" of production is the basis for social structure. Apparently, depending on the current mode of production in a given era, this will determine your political, spiritual, and intellectual pursuits in life. In other words, people are basically reactionary "sheep"...governed by their economic era. Nunes also cites Lenin often. However, I should point out here that Lenin had a certain condescending elitist attitude towards the working class. He speaks of their "false consciousness" needing guidance. Lenin-Marxist communism assumes those in the working class are incapable of changing their personal life situation without a mass revolution. I don't know where to begin in pointing out the flaws in this logic. Personal effort and insight don't seem to play into the "working" individual's capacity for change and adaptation. With communism, for example, the "benevolent" leaders decide for you what your abilities and needs are. He was also a big fan of Mao's brutal communism.

Nunes was close to the working class. It is unclear, however, if his Marxism considers capitalists as the "partying" class as opposed to the "working" class? Apparently, only the Communist leaders can think. Nonetheless, a dislike of independent thinking is evident in the communist goal of "eliminating the distinction between mental and manual labour". Allow me to venture here...that thinking can be more difficult and draining when attempting to solve certain kinds of problems. Some types of thinking are easier (and lazier), of course. Manual labor usually does not require a lot of thinking. Many find labor preferable to jobs where a lot of thinking and education is demanded. Labor generally can be done by anyone with a healthy and strong body. Some jobs might be hybrids between physical and mental work.

In any case, Nunes fails to understand that "labor value" in terms of supply and demand, is often diminished in comparison to the kind of thinking that requires a lot of extensive and expensive education. It also depends on how much demand there is for a particular type of thinking, such as fixing a dam generator providing energy to thousands. The pay discrepancy between an engineer and a warehouse worker might seem unfair to a worker in the so-called working class, however, the market demand is so much greater for a person who can guarantee thousands will have hot water, lights, functioning appliances, etc., then someone who makes sure sacks of seed are put on a truck for delivery to another business. Both have value, yet one is much greater to more people.

Merit and ambition are essential to a functioning economy. Marx's idea of "surplus value" in labor becomes a non sequitur (it doesn't follow), in light of how economics really works. If there is no demand...then there is no value...no matter how laborious the work. In management positions, thinking and figuring out processes is required so that work groups can produce something of value. When experience and education is figured into pay scales...this is not "exploitation". Nevertheless, the more I read from proponents of socialism like Ray Nunes, the more flawed it appears. Many socialists seem blinded by envy and a juvenile sense of justice.

Socialism: A Very Short Introduction (it's not that short)
Newman, Michael
Oxford University Press, Inc. New York
2005
$8.00
100
ISBN: 978-0-19-280431-0

Michael Newman's book is obviously written with much admiration for Marx and other influencers of socialism. This makes it a fairly reliable source for understanding how socialists see socialism. Being more of a scholar vs. Nunes hands-on approach, Newman does an excellent job of explaining and detailing the historical genesis and development of the concept of socialism in the last two centuries, including the Utopians, Anarchists, and the Marxists. He states that the first use of the word "socialist" was in a London co-operative magazine in 1827. He explores various contemporary issues and related movements, such as slavery and women's rights, and gives us an idea of where socialism is today.

There are some flaws in his introduction to his book. It probably prevents some people from examining the book further, which is unfortunate. He initially mischaracterizes how capitalism is viewed by capitalists. I suppose this is to be expected to some extent. For example, some of his comments on capitalism's faults demonstrates a poor understanding of cause and effect, as well as, basic human psychology. This misrepresentation is often the "strawman" for his arguments. This is illustrated in his comment that socialists reject the notion that "self-interest is the sole motivation" in economics. So do capitalists, Mr.

Newman...so do capitalists. As well, self-interest is essential to self-preservation, (it's not a bad thing) which is why humans have it.

Newman's perspective on historical events is colored by a relatively narrow field of considerations that demonstrate a bias against capitalism. The reality is that U.S. power did not defeat socialism. Socialism defeats itself. Describing Cuban Communism (a failure) and Swedish Socialist Democracy (which has lots of private ownership) as the "dominant" examples of success in socialism is a huge stretch. Newman equates socialism with the goal of egalitarianism. He fails to recognize that the pluralism and freedoms inherent in the U.S. Constitution and Declaration of Independence is far more competent in assuring reasonable egalitarian conditions for the broader population than nationalism and collectivism could ever achieve.

He sometimes speaks of the "repellant" effects of capitalism, confusing it sometimes with elements like corporatism, organized crime, and corrupt officials. What is repellant is how socialism's ultimate goal is control...which is achieved usually by insurrection. Internal revolution, violent or not, implies forcing socialism upon all citizens without any regard for their agency and independence. Ironically, Newman puts hegemony in parenthesis next to capitalism. Yet, nothing leads to hegemony more than collectivism. There may be hegemony in corporatism or a crime syndicate, but capitalism is compatible with pluralism, while socialism is compatible with hegemony.

Newman also fails to understand that the primary reason for socialism's various failures, was not because "this location" was wrong, or "that approach and timing" was not considered...but rather...when individuals were confronted with the true-to-life realities, most people recognized socialism was not an alternative to capitalism...so his historical analysis is sometimes myopic. People usually recognized right from wrong in the moment of decision. It seems to me that many socialists are incapable of comprehending the inherent evil of imposing a utopia or paradise upon others. Crystal castles might be a heaven for some and a hell for others, who prefer nature. Those who pretend to know why, and think to 'fix" such subjective humanity by imposition, are operating either on a sheltered life experience...or a diminished capacity for empathy and a lack of respect for differences in others.

When socialism speaks of "eradicating" inequality, what does it mean? Eradicating differences in people's needs and wants? People are "unequal" in many ways...it should not necessarily have a negative connotation. In the South (United States), many are content with their way of life. Even though not monetarily rich, they have land that provides their needs, freedom, family, and a happy lifestyle. Communes may be fine for the dependent in their boxed-in comfort zones, but the independent accustomed to their freedoms would fight to the bloody death to maintain those freedoms. Americans broke out of the comfort zone box long ago.

Newman also examines the philosophical dysphoria in democratic socialism after its split with communism. The reality is that socialism is inherently undemocratic. The phrase "democratic socialism" is an oxymoron and a contradiction. Their attempts at an ambiguous equality is without any underlying logic, purpose, or focus. It is a mechanical shell devoid of soul, and isn't based on anything real beyond materialistic fairness...whatever that means...as different people value different material differently. He downplays the horrors of abolition expressed in the brutal doctrine of the Communist Manifesto. The non-chantalant atmospheric of Newman's writing about violent events can seem indifferent and signal support of such actions in future activity. Newman's mischaracterizes socialism as "mixed results" in light of its blatant failures.

Newman has also mischaracterized capitalism as having a "ruling" class in the same sense as slavery and feudalism. It is not true, of course. There are corporate thugs, corrupt politicians, and organized crime cartels...but these illegal elements are in no sense the legal "rulers" of capitalism. There are none. What an individual makes from applying capitalism is its only "ruling" criteria.

The Communist Manifesto
Karl Marx

This is not an easy document to read. It is soaring rhetoric full of droning vitriol and logic errors. It is also what I would call "lazily" pedantic. It is basically in four parts. The first part defines the relationship between the untrustworthy bourgeoisie (middle class) creating superstructures, and the oppressed proletariat (working class) providing the economic substructure for the middle class. The second part examines the relationship between the benevolent communists and the inferior proletariat. The third part is the different kinds of misguided socialisms. The fourth part defines communism in relation to these misguided opposition parties. Practically every paragraph contains or implies multiple logic errors and unsubstantiated generalizations.

For example, "the Bourgeoisie (Marx's term that pertains to the property-owning middle-class) cannot exist without constantly revolutionizing the instruments of production...". To illustrate just a few problems with statements like this...bourgeoisie is a term made up by Marx to create a simplistic distinction between rich owners and poor workers (the proletarians). The archaic terms themselves don't reflect a broader reality of social strata, not even in his day. People by nature explore, discover, and invent. It's not a bad thing. Some do it better than others...it's nothing to be jealous of. Rather, we should encourage such for everyone's benefit. Apart from its false assumptions about a division of two classes, it is simply not a true statement. As well, plenty of so-called "bourgeoisie" could care less about "revolutionizing instruments of production". He is suggesting a mass planned hegemony where it doesn't exist.

The Communist Manifesto is full of these "soaring" whimsical extrapolations based on his own false or half-truth generalizations. If anything, the manifesto itself invents and contributes to his so-called class warfare. He writes that capitalism is "prone to crisis". It is my understanding that just being alive is prone to crisis. If this is a big deal, I would suggest that socialism is prone to war, death, destruction, imprisonment, etc. Which is more serious? When so-called "structural inequalities" exist in a free society it is usually due to criminal and unethical influences. This will be true of any kind of society, including a socialist society. The difference is that in a free capitalist society, the criminals are more likely to be caught and prosecuted for their crimes, no matter their class or status in society. In a socialist society, the controllers are well protected from this...because they are in "total" control. Americans have little problem with convicting their presidents of crimes, not so in totalitarian states and dictatorships. Total war is usually the only way to remove these tyrants. The abstract illusion that "the people" will be in control of a nationalized and centralized economy ignores physical and psychological reality.

No doubt Marx observed exploitations and injustices just as the rest of us do. It happens in every strata of society. However, no so-called "class" has a monopoly on it. Marx is great at pointing out all the terrible events happening around him and in the world, however, he is not so good at citing actual cause and effect. In other words, his emotional content isn't really guided by any analytical accumanship. He sees results...ignores or assumes causation (it's all because of the bourgeoisie). This approach will create cynicism in just about anyone. Instead of seeing active responsible people trying to make the world more livable, broad, and free for all, he sees them as the nefarious culprits of change. Change is scary...therefore, not good. Well, as usual...it depends on what is changed, and why. This is what socialism is all about. Fear of change, fear of personal responsibility, uncertainty, and fear of growth. It must be stopped!

Marx's fear and hate of the affluent is based on affluence itself, since his argument is to group them all together. Anyone who dares to become affluent is automatically part of the problem...so it is not the bourgeoisie per se...but the idea of having affluence is bad. It becomes a ridiculous argument. Why is Marx so vehemently full of vitriol toward the middle-class in his manifesto? He grew up in a comfortable middle class existence. When his father died the family lost income and he became poorer. He was frivolous in his youthful pursuits and his academics and his writings were not published in his lifetime. He had perpetual health problems exacerbated by smoking and drinking and was always poor. I mention this in very light detail to point out it was under such conditions that he labeled, and then attacked the affluent, which I believe was in bitterness. I suspect he was just trying to find a relevant place and purpose for himself in the wider world. The details are downplayed and smoothed over by the hardcore socialists of today.

Socialism:
The Failed Idea that Never Dies
Kristian Niemietz
IEA Institute of Economic Affairs
Great Britain 2019
374 pages
27.00
Interactive PDF/book
ISBN: 978-0-255-36771-4

Dr. Niemietz explores the history and development of socialism with statements from proponents, ex-proponents, and opposers...along with his analysis. He includes a number of studies and charts on public opinion and such. Niemietz also briefly chronicles the excursions of western intellectuals into socialist countries. He then gives a brief history on the various failed attempts at socialism throughout the last two centuries, including the Soviet Union, China, Cuba, North Korea, Albania, etc.

In regards to capitalism, he points out that there are four basic misconceptions by most socialists. (1) There is a "knee jerk" condemnation of profit motive. Anti-profit moralism is part of the socialist mind-set. (2) A false assumption that the public sector is driven by altruistic..."the common good"...motives. (studies show instead that self-interests exist equally in the public and political spheres). (3) A false assumption there is a conflict between needs and profit. (4) A false notion that nationalism brings industry under democratic control, making it accountable to the public. If millions own something, how would they control it?

Newman mentions that "socialists tend to escape into abstraction". He considers that the idea of public ownership is a mirage, and the idea of "the people", a romanticized abstraction. This explains, he says, why socialists can only use nice soundbites, but can't explain how it would work. He refers to Seldon's statement that "the machinery of social control has never been devised" I suspect that is because you are not supposed to control people? Niemietz's book, one would think, should be enough to convince people of the failure of socialism...however, I suspect it will not be. Nevertheless, combined with other books such as mine, hopefully it will be enough to influence future American society to avoid foolish attempts at socio-economic collectivization, misguided centralization, and the nationalization of industry.

Socialism:
An Economic and Sociological Analysis
Ludwig von Mises
New Haven Yale University Press
1951
593 pages
PDF

Mises book is considered a seminal work by capitalists and many others. He states "...about the middle of the nineteenth century, it seemed the ideal of Socialism had been disposed of. Science had demonstrated its worthlessness by means of strict logic and its supporters were unable to produce a single effective counter-argument. It was at this moment that Marx appeared. Adept as he was in the hegelian dialectic - a system easy of abuse by those who seek to dominate thought by arbitrary flights of fancy and metaphysical verbosity - he was not slow in finding a way out of the dilemma in which socialists found themselves." Mises identifies Marx's three procedures of attack as (1) deny the universality of logic, (2) expropriate the expropriators (the negation of negation), and (3) no proposals would ever be submitted for the construction of the Socialist Promised Land. Since the coming of socialism was inevitable, science should renounce attempts to determine its nature. This excused socialism of any self-accountability and found immediate and complete acceptance by socialists world-wide. The dream could go on. The reality of socialism is far in the future and remains undefined.

Mises joins others from various political ideologies and academic disciplines in criticisms of Marxism. "These include general criticisms about a lack of internal consistency, criticisms related to historical materialism, that it is a type of historical determinism, the necessity of suppression of individual rights, issues with the implementation of communism and economic issues such as the *distortion or absence of price signals* and reduced incentives. In addition, empirical and epistemological problems are frequently identified." (*Wikipedia, undated*) It is indeed sophistry because most do not understand enough of economics to identify its critical flaws. Mises continues "...not Marxists alone, but most of those who emphatically declare themselves anti-Marxists, think entirely on Marxist lines and have adopted Marx's arbitrary, unconfirmed and easily refutable dogmas."

Mises further states "Marxism is thus the most radical of all reactions against the reign of scientific thought over life and action, established by Rationalism. It is against logic, against science and against the activity of thought and inquiry, especially as it is applied to the institutions and workings of a socialist economy." "Bolshevists (Russian Communists) persistently tell us that religion is opium for the people. Marxism is indeed opium for those who might take to thinking and must therefore be weaned from it. Mises writes "Marx's so-called "scientific socialism" tells us there is an historical evolution...an obscure force from which we cannot escape leads humanity step by step to higher planes of social and moral being. History is a progressive process of purification, with perfection, in the form of Socialism, at the end." If this isn't supernatural nonsense, what is?

This determinism is based on Marx's concept of historical materialism, free will and choice by humans play no role. A philosophy that seeks the abolition of religion and secular science, bases itself on a mystical and material ideology. Go figure. Mises states..."according to the Marxist conception, one's social condition determines one's way of thought." Here is a sentence from the Communist Manifesto. "But Communism abolishes eternal truths, it abolishes all religion, and all morality, instead constituting them on a new basis: it therefore acts in contradiction to all past historical experience." All of material history is abolished because it determined people's way of thinking. In essence, a certain material existence and social experience is a bad thing because it determines how you think. And, naturally, that is not going to apply to the communist leaders...because they are above...um...thinking? Marxism is Metaphysical gobbledegook.

Bibliography

1. Vocabulary.com (undated), https://www.vocabulary.com/diction-
   ary/federalism
2. Wikipedia (undated), *Pluralism*, retrieved from en.wikipedia.org
   Nov. 16, 2017
3. *The Declaration of Independence and the Constitution of the United
   States* (1998) by the Cato Institute, 1000 Massachusetts Ave.,
   N.W. Washington, D.C. 20001, (see Preface)
4. Britannica.com/topic/*The-Founding-Fathers-Deism-and-Christian-
   ity-1272214*
5. Thoreau, Henry David (1843), *On Walden Pond*, retrieved from
   thoreau.library.ucsb.edu/thoreau_walden.html Mar. 13, 2019
6. Knudsen, Thorbjorn; Swedburg, Richard (2009), *Capitalistic En-
   trepreneurship: Making Profit through the Unmaking of Economic Or-
   ders*, (abstract), Capitalism and Society, Vol. 4, Iss. 2, Art. 3, (go
   down to "Schumpter on Combinations")
7. https://fitsmallbusiness.com/entrepreneurship-statistics/ retrieved
   Mar. 13, 2019
8. *The Politics Book*, dk publishing, 2013
9. http://www.let.rug.nl/usa/documents/1786-1800/the-federalist-
   papers/ retrieved Mar. 13, 2019 (Federalist 10)

10. https://www.stlouisfed.org/education/economic-lowdown-podcast-series/episode-12-price-signals

11. Gimenez, Eric Holt (Dec. 18, 2014), *We Already Grow Enough Food For 10 Billion People - and Still Can't End Hunger*, retrieved from www.huffingtonpost.com on Nov. 15, 2017

12. Friedman, Milton (1977) Nobel Laureate, *Fairness*, Hoover Institution.

13. Niemietz, Kristian, 2019, iea.org.uk/publications/socialism-the-failed-idea-that-never-dies/

14. Lee, Zachary (May 21, 2013), *What Does Church and State Really mean?*, retrieved on November 15, 2017 from www.tvcresources.net

15. United Nations, https://en.wikipedia.org/wiki/*United_Nations*

16. Google Dictionary, *Sharia*, retrieved March 2018

17. https://sustainabledevelopment.un.org/outcomedocuments/agenda21, retrieved Mar. 13, 2019.

18. https://www.urbandictionary.com/define.php?term=Corporatism, 2010.

19. Smith, Adam (1776), *The Wealth of Nations*, Adam Smith Institute, retrieved on February 21, 2013 from www.adamsmith.org/adam-smith (Book IV, Chapter II, paragraph IX)

20. Tocqueville, Alexis de, 1835, www.learningtogive.org/resources/enlightened-self-interest

21. https://en.wikipedia.org/wiki/Ludwig_von_Mises, undated, *praxeology*

22. Marx, Karl (1848), The Communist Manifesto, *IV. Position of the Communists in relation to the Various Existing Opposition Parties*, Melbourne School of Continental Philosophy (Winter 2009)

23. Wikipedia, https://en.wikipedia.org/wiki/Cultural_hegemony, retrieved Mar. 13, 2019.

24. Wikipedia, https://en.wikipedia.org/wiki/Modern_liberalism_in_the_United_States

25. Mises, Ludwig Von, 1951, *Socialism: An Economic and Sociological Analysis*, New Haven Yale University Press.

26. Adams, John (1798), *From John Adams to Massachusetts Militia, 11 October 1798*, retrieved from founders.archives.gov., Nov. 16, 2017

27. Rossiter, Lyle Jr., M.D., *On the Madness of Modern Liberalism*, retrieved from www.libertymind.com, on Nov. 16, 2017

28. Weaver, Henry Grady (1999), *The Mainspring of Human Progress*, retrieved on Nov. 16, 2017 from admin.fee.org., (PDF) The Foundation for Economic Education Irvington-on-Hudson, New York

29. Sowell, Thomas (2010), *Intellectuals and Society*, Basic Books, A Member of the Perseus Books Group, New York retrieved Nov. 16, 2017

30. Johnson, Paul (2007), *Intellectuals: From Marx and Tolstoy to Sartre and Chomsky*, Publisher Harper Perennial

31. Wolfe, Tom (2000), *Way More than Luck: Boston University Commencement*, pg. 60, retrieved Nov. 16, 2017

32. Adorno, T. Horkheimer, M., (1972) *Dialectic of Enlightenment*, Frankfurt School, rationalwiki.org

33. Alinsky, Saul (1971), *Rules for Radicals*, Random House, retrieved on Nov. 17, 2014 www.google.com, Summary.

34. time.com/4501910/president-obama-united-nations-speech-transcript/ ("Powerful nations contest the constraints placed upon them by international law...I believe that as imperfect as they are...International laws that we have forged remain the firmist foundation for human progress in this century"..."*it does not require succumbing to a soulless capitalism*"..."that benefits only the few"..."...more successful when we close the gap between the rich and poor...")

35. Diagnostic and Statistical Manual of Mental Disorders, (2000), *Antisocial Personality Disorders*, APA...pp. 701-706.

36. Burns, Nick (2018) *Effective Self-Justification: Charity and the Crisis of Political Service at Stanford*, 2018 The Stanford Review.

37. Wikipedia, *Genocide Convention*, undated

38. Wikipedia Free Encyclopedia (undated)
    https://en.wikipedia.org/wiki/*Battle_of_Stalingrad*

39. Steinburg, Laurence, et al (October 2009), *Are Adolescents Less Mature than Adults?*, American Psychologist (PDF), retrieved on February 20, 2013 from
    www.wisspd.org/htm/ATPracGuides/Training/ProgMatertials/.../AALMA.pdf

40. Vygotsky, Lev S. (1934), *Thought and Language*, Cambridge, Mass., MIT press, 1986, pgs. 252-53 (start with second paragraph/consider book summation)

41. The Oxford English Unabridged Dictionary (1989), *Law*, Clarendon Press, Oxford, England, Rand McNally & Company, Taurton, Illinois. (Multi-volume used in defining author's levels of learning)

42. Snopes: Fact Check. https://www.snopes.com/fact-check/facts-about-slavery/, retrieved Mar. 19, 2019.

43. https://en.wikipedia.org/wiki/*Native_American_disease_and_epidemics*

44. https://www.npr.org/sections/thetwo-way/2016/09/27/495627997/u-s-government-to-pay-492-million-to-17-american-indian-tribes

45. https://en.m.wikipedia.org/wiki/Indian_reservation

46. Wikipedia, *Habeas Corpus*, undated

47. The Oxford English Dictionary (1989), https://en.oxforddictionaries.com/*definition/law*

48. Benson, Robert W. (1985), *The End of Legalese*, New York University School of Law, retrieved on February 22, 2013 from
    www.law.nyu.edu/Journals/.../issues/ECM.PRO.070368

49. https://www.google.com/search?hl=en&ei=3VCTXO6QBszTwSAloLYAQ&q=Google+Dictionary+define+anarchy&oq=Google+Dictionary+define+anarchy

50. Free Online Dictionary (undated), *Politics*, Farlex, retrieved on February 20, 2013 from www.thefreedictionary.com/politics

51. Wilcox, L., 2017, *Examining the Relationship between extremism and terrorism*, retrieved on Feb. 26, 2018, https://medium.com/.../examining-the-relationship-between-extremism-and-terrorism

52. Wiktionary (undated), *-logy*, Wikipedia.org, retrieved on February 22, 2013 from en.wiktionary.org/wiki/-logy

53. Office of Research Integrity: Piltdown events/Fraud https://facultydevelopment.massgeneral.org/orcd/pdf/20150429RCR*ResearchIntegrity_presentation.pdf*

54. Shuttleworth, Martyn (2008), *Paradigm Shift*, Explorable, retrieved on February 24, 2013 from www.explorable.com/paradigm-shift

55. Oxford Dictionaries (2013), *Fundamentalism*, Oxford University Press, retrieved on February 28, 2013 from oxforddictionaries.com/definition/english/fundamentalism

56. Wikipedia (2013), *Reification (fallacy)*, Wikipedia, The Free Encyclopedia, retrieved on February 26, 2013 from en.wikipedia.org/wiki/Reification_(fallacy)

57. Covey, Stephen R. (2004), The 7 Habits of Highly Effective People: *Restoring the Character Ethic*, New York: Simon and Schuster, c1989

www.ingramcontent.com/pod-product-compliance
Lightning Source LLC
Chambersburg PA
CBHW070714250726
48662CB00001B/402

9 781646 103522